D0896899

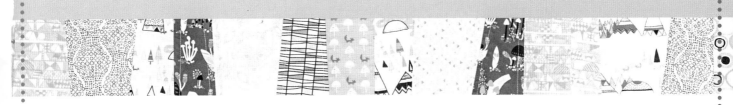

Quilt As-You-Go
Made Modern

FRESH TECHNIQUES FOR BUSY QUILTERS

Jera Brandvig

stashBOOKS.

an imprint of C&T Publishing

Text copyright © 2014 by Jera Brandvig

Photography and Artwork copyright © 2014 by C&T Publishing, Inc.

Publisher: Amy Marson

Creative Director: Gailen Runge

Art Director: Kristy Zacharias

Editor: Karla Menaugh

Technical Editors: Julie Waldman and Nanette S. Zeller

Cover Designer: April Mostek

Book Designer: Katie McIntosh

Production Coordinator: Zinnia Heinzmann

Production Editor: Joanna Burgarino

Illustrator: Mary E. Flynn

Photo Assistant: Mary Peyton Peppo

Photo Stylist: Lauren Toker

Styled photography by Nissa Brehmer and instructional photography by Diane Pedersen, unless otherwise noted

Published by Stash Books, an imprint of C&T Publishing, Inc., P.O. Box 1456, Lafayette, CA 94549

Library of Congress Cataloging-in-Publication Data

Brandvig, Jera, 1985-

 Quilt as-you-go made modern : fresh techniques for busy quilters / Jera Brandvig.

  pages cm

 ISBN 978-1-60705-901-1 (soft cover)

1. Patchwork quilts. 2. Patchwork--Patterns. 3. Quilting--Patterns. 4. Machine sewing--Technique. I. Title.

 TT835.B6634 2014

 746.46--dc23

                          2014004193

Printed in the USA

20 19 18 17

Photo by Keith Russell

Dedication

Dedicated to my husband, Ben, who bought me my first sewing machine even though I was terrified to use one. I don't think he knew what he was getting us into! Thank you for being encouraging, supportive, and loving for every step of the way, in both my quilting endeavors and life in general. Love you forever.

Contents

Introduction   4

Getting Started   8

Quilt As-You-Go Techniques   16

Projects   *36*

Solstice Parade   38

Rainy Days   44

Red Square   48

Chief Sealth   54

Queen Anne Steps   60

Reversible Table Runner   64

Pillow Sham   68

Ballard Blocks   74

The Emerald City   80

Cascade Range   86

Portage Bay   92

Triple Shot Sampler   96

Finish It!   102

About the Author   110

Resources   111

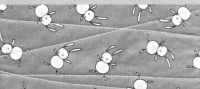

Introduction

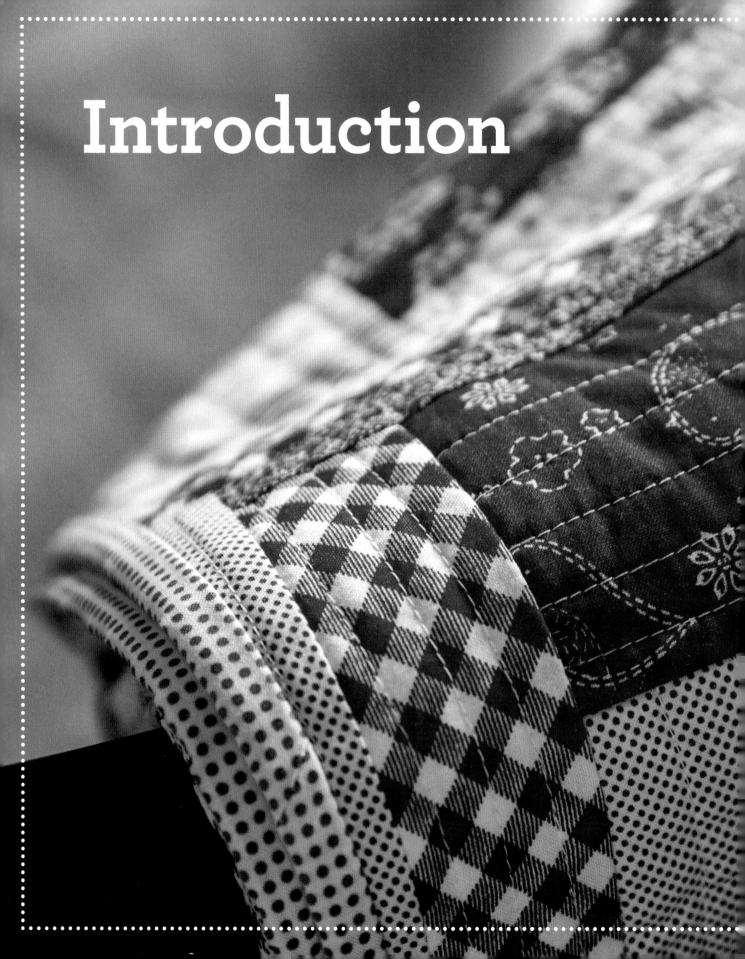

Break free from following the "rules" and embrace your inner creativity to make a one-of-a-kind quilt!

After having my son, the only time I had left to quilt was late at night, when the last thing I should be doing is handling a rotary cutter and making precise measurements. When it is that late, I'm just not all there, if you know what I mean. My style of quilting had to adapt to my lifestyle.

Quilting as-you-go allows you to be truly creative and expressive with your quilting. Free yourself from following precise patterns and make your quilt your way! Take a break from maneuvering a large quilt sandwich through your sewing machine. This technique allows you to intricately quilt onto small and manageable blocks. It is a fresh, fun, and simpler-than-it-sounds technique that will change the way you quilt.

My philosophy on quilting has always been to keep it simple, yet creative, and to have fun during the whole process. When there's a step you dread or that intimidates you, that is when you end up with a pile of unfinished projects. The quilt as-you-go technique is great for the beginning quilter because it is a very forgiving technique, and it is also excellent for a seasoned quilter who wants to learn a fresh approach.

You can thank my son for making me "quilt outside the box." The quilt in this photo is *Solstice Parade* (page 38).

Photo by Jera Brandvig

Detail of *Rainy Days* (page 44)

Photo by Jera Brandvig

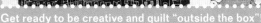

Get ready to be creative and quilt "outside the box"!

WHAT IS QUILT AS-YOU-GO?

My style of quilting as-you-go is similar to foundation/paper piecing, except the fabric is pieced directly onto small batting blocks instead of paper. This technique is a style of improvisational quilting, but you can use it to make quilts as abstract or structured as you want.

Traditional Quilting vs. Quilting As-You-Go

With traditional quilting, the first step involves precisely measuring and cutting your fabric, followed by piecing together your quilt top. Next, you baste the quilt by sandwiching the batting between the quilt top and quilt backing fabric; this is all held together by hundreds of pins you have meticulously placed to keep the layers of the "quilt sandwich" from shifting and falling apart. Lastly, you roll the quilt sandwich up as best as you can, and feed it through your sewing machine to quilt it. For many (myself included), maneuvering a large piece of material through a sewing machine can get frustrating and physically tiresome.

When you quilt as-you-go, you piece the quilt top together directly onto smaller pieces of batting, which allows you to bypass quilting a large quilt sandwich all at once. When you quilt directly onto small and manageable batting blocks, quilting is a completely different—and refreshing—experience! After you have finished quilting the blocks and assembling them, you need only add backing fabric and binding.

Advantages of Quilting As-You-Go

- You work with small and manageable pieces, which means you can quilt more intricately without the physical strain and frustration of feeding a large quilt sandwich through a sewing machine.

- The improvisational style of quilting is mentally stimulating. You are creating something brand-new that is *all you*. I guarantee you that no two quilts will be the same!

- Quilt as-you-go is great for on-the-go moms or anyone with a busy schedule. You can easily start and stop with this style of quilting. Anything left half done will already be quilted onto the batting, making it easy to pick up where you left off.

- You will complete a quilt in no time because you are literally quilting as-you-go directly onto the batting! This means fewer unfinished projects piling up!

- Easily finish your own quilts and save money on long-arm quilting services. Use all that money you saved to buy more fabric!

I'm absolutely thrilled to be sharing this with you, and I hope you'll get as much creative inspiration and as many finished quilts as I have from this fresh and fun technique!

Happy quilting as-you-go!

"Learn the rules like a pro, so you can break them like an artist." —Anonymous

Photo by Jera Brandvig

Paige, my sewing buddy and "#1 quilt fan," was happy as a clam when I finished *Salmon Run* (page 47).

Getting Started

SUPPLIES

In addition to your sewing machine, you will need some other basic supplies. See Resources (page 111) for information about where to buy these products.

Cutting Mats

- 24″ × 36″ cutting mat

Use this for cutting the batting and fabric. I don't have a big crafting area, so I usually tuck my mat behind my sewing table. When I need it, I lay it out on my dining table or even the floor. It is not ideal (hey, not everyone has Martha Stewart's crafting room, right?), but it works! If you do have to stash your mat when it's not in use, be sure to keep it flat against the wall— or under your bed—so it doesn't develop wobbles.

- 14″ × 14″ rotating cutting mat

This mat rotates 360°, which makes squaring up blocks (pages 22 and 23) faster and prevents awkward cutting positions. It is one of the tools I use the most. I use Fiskars cutting mats and rotary cutters because they are good quality and affordable.

Rotary Cutters

- 45mm rotary cutter

Use this for cutting fabric.

- 60mm rotary cutter

This large cutter is the right size for cutting batting.

Cutting Rulers

- 3″ × 24″ or 6″ × 24″ ruler

Use these longer rulers to cut batting and fabric.

- 9½″ or 12½″ square ruler

Use these to quickly square up your blocks (pages 22 and 23).

Tabletop Ironing Board

When you quilt as-you-go, you iron after sewing every seam, so it is helpful to have a small tabletop ironing board near your sewing machine.

Even-feed walking foot

TIP · · · · · · · · · · ·

You may find that you can
get away without using an
even-feed walking foot when
quilting your blocks. Try it
out; if you get puckering,
then an even-feed walking
foot will solve the problem.

· · · · · · · · · · · · · · · · · ·

Even-Feed Walking Foot

I use a walking foot to sew blocks together and a regular presser foot
to quilt the blocks. Each sewing machine has feed dogs that move the
fabric from the bottom. An even-feed walking foot adds feed dogs to
the top as well. With feed dogs on the top and bottom of the fabric,
the layers of the quilt feed evenly through the machine, preventing any
puckering. Using the foot makes it easier to sew through thick layers of
fabric and batting. (Some machines have built-in "dual feed" capability;
if you have this, you will not need a walking foot—just make sure the
dual feed is engaged.)

Fabric Scissors

In addition to quilting as-you-go, you will also be cutting as-you-go
(page 17), so be sure to have a good pair of fabric scissors on hand.

Thread

I suggest using a neutral-colored thread that blends into your fabric. If
you use a colorful thread, it can compete with the fabric on your quilt
and make the design look busy. For all of the quilts in this book I used
white, 100% cotton Essential Thread by Connecting Threads, which is
affordable and high quality. This technique uses a lot of thread because
you use it for both piecing and quilting.

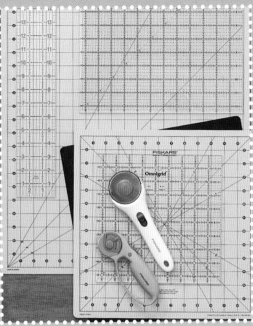

Curved Safety Pins

The curve allows the pin to pop right back up through your fabric, which will make basting a quilt so much faster and easier.

Needle-Punched Batting

With this technique, you will piece the fabric and quilt it directly onto batting squares. During any kind of quilting, whether quilt as-you-go or traditional quilting, your batting will stretch or warp. It is the fluffy insulation that enables a quilt to be warm and cozy, so that is just the nature of the material!

To deal with this, I buy needle-punched batting and cut the batting large enough to compensate for any warping.

The fibers in needle-punched batting are held together by being punched with thousands of tiny needles (as opposed to with resins and glue), which creates a lower-loft and dense sheet of batting that feels almost fleece-like. It is easy to work with, and I have found this material to have the least amount of warping.

Choose a needle-punched batting that is at least 80% cotton. Blends that have too much polyester may melt slightly if you need to press seams open (page 28).

My favorite two batting brands:

- 100% cotton needle-punched batting by Pellon. The Legacy line of needle-punched batting from Pellon is wonderful too.

- 87.5% cotton / 12.5% polyester Warm & White by the Warm Company.

WORKING WITH BATTING

Bigger Is Better

The general rule of thumb is to cut the batting 1″ bigger than the squared, or trimmed, block size.

How to Cut Batting

1. Fold the batting at the width until it fits on the cutting mat. Make sure the folds are as straight as you can get them. If you start with a big sheet of batting, roll up the extra batting and unravel it as you cut, or trim it to a more manageable size before you start. Flatten out the folds as much as possible, and align the folds to a horizontal line on the cutting mat.

2. Using a rotary cutter and ruler, trim the uneven ends off an end of the batting so that the width of the batting is at a 90° angle with the horizontal line on the cutting mat.

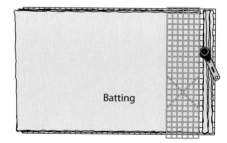

Batting

3. Cut long batting strips the width of the squares you will need.

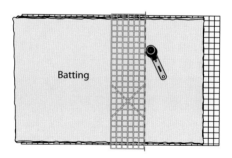

Batting

4. Subcut squares from the batting strips.

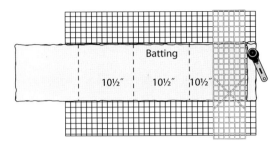

PLANNING YOUR QUILT SIZE

How Many Blocks Will You Need?

The number of blocks you will need depends on the quilt size and how large the blocks will be.

Use the Quilt Size Guides (page 14) to see how many blocks you need to make a baby, lap, twin, full/queen, or king-size quilt. For example, if you are making a pattern where the finished block measures 12″ × 12″ and you want to make a lap-size quilt, you will need 30 batting squares measuring 13½″ × 13½″ each.

The majority of the projects in this book use 9″ and 12″ finished blocks, which is why we have these specific guides. You can make any size blocks you want, however, simply by cutting the batting 1″ larger than the trimmed block size (or 1½″ larger than the finished block size).

These are loose guidelines because standard quilt sizes tend to vary. Easily customize the size of your quilt by adding or subtracting rows of blocks.

Quilt Size Guide for
9″ Finished Blocks

Cut batting squares 10½″ × 10½″. The blocks will be 9½″ × 9½″ after they are squared up.

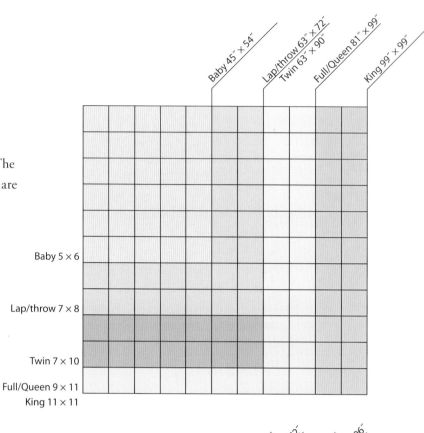

Baby 45″ × 54″
Lap/throw 63″ × 72″
Twin 63″ × 90″
Full/Queen 81″ × 99″
King 99″ × 99″

Baby 5 × 6
Lap/throw 7 × 8
Twin 7 × 10
Full/Queen 9 × 11
King 11 × 11

Quilt Size Guide for
12″ Finished Blocks

Cut batting squares 13½″ × 13½″. The blocks will be 12½″ × 12½″ after they are squared up.

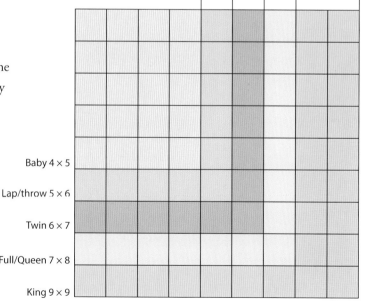

Baby 48″ × 60″
Lap/throw 60″ × 72″
Twin 72″ × 90″
Full/Queen 84″ × 96″
King 108″ × 108″

Baby 4 × 5
Lap/throw 5 × 6
Twin 6 × 7
Full/Queen 7 × 8
King 9 × 9

Not Sure How Much Batting Yardage to Buy?

Use the diagram to see how many 10½″ or 13½″ squares you can cut.

Batting by the yard (90″ wide)								
	1 yard	1¼ yards	1½ yards	1¾ yards	2 yards	2¼ yards	2½ yards	2¾ yards	3 yards
10½″ squares	24	32	40	48	48	56	64	72	80
13½″ squares	12	18	24	24	30	36	36	42	48

Pre-packaged batting					
	Craft 34″ × 45″	Crib 45″ × 60″	Twin 72″ × 90″	Full 81″ × 96″	Queen 90″ × 108″	King 120″ × 120″
10½″ squares	12	20	48	63	80	121
13½″ squares	6	12	30	42	48	64

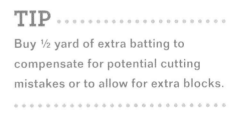

TIP

Buy ½ yard of extra batting to compensate for potential cutting mistakes or to allow for extra blocks.

Quilt As-You-Go Techniques

I encourage you to read this chapter thoroughly before starting a project. You will find lots of helpful tidbits that will allow you to use this technique at its best. Enjoy!

CUT AS-YOU-GO!

When you quilt as-you-go, the cutting is simple and fast, which allows you to start quilting right away.

Start by rotary cutting strips × the width of the fabric. These cuts typically don't have to be exact. The rest of the cutting is done right at your sewing machine using fabric scissors.

TIP

Cutting as-you-go works because quilt as-you-go is a forgiving technique that does not require precise cuts. You decide which prints you want to cut and quilt as you piece your block together.

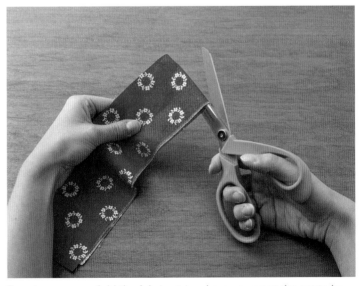

To cut as-you-go, fold the fabric strip where you want the cut to be made and use fabric scissors to cut at the fold.

TIP · · · · · · · · · · · · · · · · · ·

Change the needle position on your sewing machine so that the tip of the needle is ¼″ from the edge of the presser foot. To sew a ¼″ seam, guide the presser foot along the edge of the fabric. If your machine does not have a needle-width adjuster, use a ¼″ guide foot. See Resources (page 111).

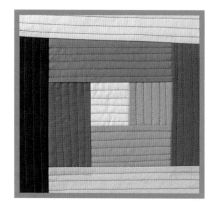

Making a Log Cabin–Style Block

Learn to make a traditional Log Cabin–style block using the quilt as-you-go technique. You will quilt straight lines onto each patch, building a beautiful quilting pattern that will look like it took hours to create!

Materials

- A batting square 1″ bigger than the block's trim size

- Fabric strips 2½″ × the width of fabric

Sewing

Use a ¼″ seam allowance for piecing and quilt assembly unless specified otherwise.

1. Use fabric scissors to cut a square from the end of a fabric strip. It is okay if it is not an exact square. Use the cut as-you-go technique (page 17) when trimming all strips.

2. Place the fabric square in the center of the batting square. Quilt a design onto the square, using straight lines.

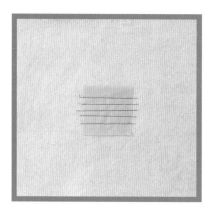

3. From a different strip, cut a square approximately the same size as the square you just quilted. Place the second square on top of the first, right sides together, aligning an edge that is perpendicular to the quilting lines on the first square. Sew along that edge.

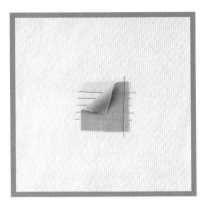

4. Press the seam open, doing your best to avoid ironing the batting. Quilt the second square directly onto the batting using straight lines parallel to the new seam.

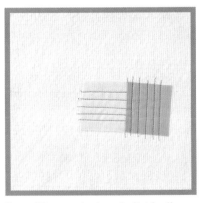

By quilting each piece individually, you will create a beautiful and intricate labyrinth of quilting.

TIPS

• When quilting, start and end the stitching line off the fabric and on the batting. There is no need to backstitch. Don't put an important part of the quilting design in the outer ¼″ of the fabric, though, because this section will become the seam allowance.

• Use a stitch length of 3.5 on a scale of 0–5. This length is not small enough to create bunching, but also not long enough to be a basting stitch.

• If the fabric starts to bunch or pucker, try using an even-feed walking foot (page 10).

• Get into the habit of trimming the trailing threads. If your sewing machine has an automatic thread cutter that quickly snips the thread with a push of the button, then you are in luck! You'll soon find that button to be your new best friend.

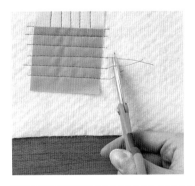

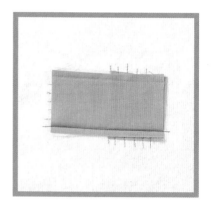 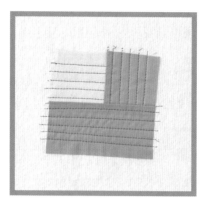 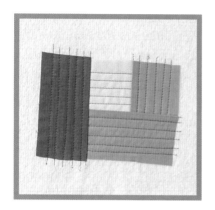

5. From a third strip, cut a length to match the 2 squares that you just quilted. Place the third strip on top of the first 2, right sides facing together. Align an edge along the length of the first 2 pieces and sew.

6. Press open. Quilt straight lines parallel to the new seam.

7. From a fourth strip, cut a length to match the width of the first and third pieces. Use the same process to attach and quilt it, stitching the quilted lines parallel to the new seam.

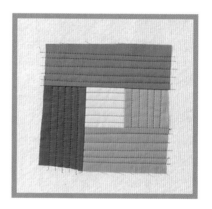 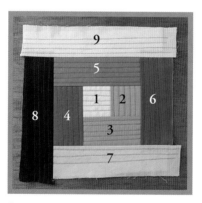 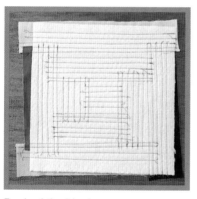

Front of a block covered with pieced, quilted strips

Back of the block

8. Repeat with a fifth strip.

9. Continue to add strips and quilt each with lines parallel to the new seams. Build on the central patchwork until you cover the batting with pieced and quilted strips. In this example, I added fabric in a clockwise direction. You will have extra fabric around the edge of the batting. You can trim and square up the block later.

TIP

When you start quilting your fabric may warp—this is expected. To help straighten your pieces and keep everything "square" looking, simply attach your additional pieces so they run parallel or perpendicular to the seams already on the block.

TIP

For most of the block construction, you have started and ended all stitching *on* the batting. Once you reach the edge of the batting, you will have to start and stop the stitching lines *off* the batting. In most cases, you can keep stitching through the extra fabric hanging off the edge of the batting.

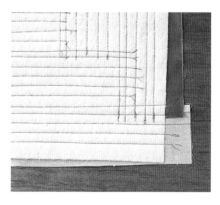

Four Simple Quilt As-You-Go Guidelines

1. When you piece fabric onto the batting, the pieces have to build upon the initial patchwork. Do not quilt one piece to the batting and then add another strip off in a random corner. Add to the initial fabric piece so that it grows bigger until patchwork eventually covers the entire batting square.

2. When you add a strip, cut it the same length as the edge where it will be attached. If you add a shorter or longer strip, you will create an angle in the patchwork that you cannot piece over with a single ¼" seam allowance.

3. Start and end the stitching line on the batting when possible. When you get to the outer edge of the batting, start and end the stitches on the excess fabric hanging off the edge of the batting. There is no need to backstitch.

4. If you plan to quilt each piece individually, the general rule of thumb is to make the quilting lines run parallel to the new seam. See Quilting Techniques (page 24–27) for other quilting options.

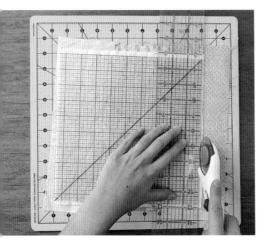

To use a plastic template, align a ruler with the edge of the template and cut.

TIP • • • • • • • • • • • • • • • • •

A rotating cutting mat will make squaring up your blocks a cinch. If you don't own one yet, go treat yourself! It will be a useful tool for both quilt as-you-go and traditional quilting.

• •

SQUARING UP THE BLOCKS

After you have completely covered the batting, the block is ready to be trimmed to a perfect square ½″ larger than the finished size of the block. This is called squaring up the block.

I highly recommend using a rotating cutting mat because you can efficiently trim all four sides of a block without having to pick up and reposition the block. It will be easier to trim the blocks if you have a square ruler the same size as the trimmed block. In this book, the trimmed block sizes are usually 9½″ or 12½″ square.

An alternative to buying square rulers is to cut a square of template plastic to match the trim size of the block. To use the template as a guide, align a cutting ruler along the edge of the template and trim with a rotary cutter.

Improvisational Square-Up Technique

Use this method if you are *not* trying to cut the front of the block a specific way. This method works well for blocks that have an improvisational or abstract look.

1. Place the block on the cutting mat with the batting side facing you.

2. Position the square ruler or template on the block so that it is within the batting and as centered as possible.

3. Use a rotary cutter to trim the excess fabric on all 4 sides.

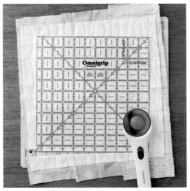

With the batting facing you, position the ruler within the batting and trim all 4 sides.

Squared-up block

Precise Square-Up Technique

Use this technique when you want the front of the block trimmed a specific way. In this method, you will finish squaring up the block with the front of the block facing you.

1. Place the block on the cutting mat with the batting side facing you. Align a ruler with the edge of the batting and trim the excess fabric from all 4 sides.

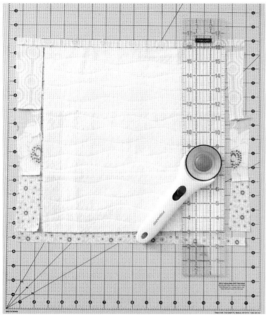

With the batting facing you, trim the excess fabric outside the batting.

2. Turn the block over so the front faces up. Position the square ruler or template to your specific needs.

3. Use a rotary cutter to trim excess fabric on all 4 sides.

Turn the block front side up.
Position the ruler and trim all 4 sides.

Squared-up block

QUILTING TECHNIQUES

Quilting each piece onto the batting individually is just one option for how to quilt a block. Here are some other ideas.

No Quilting

This block was pieced directly onto the batting, and that was it. The result is similar to stitch-in-the-ditch quilting. To add more quilting, you could always quilt an allover design on the entire block after it is pieced.

Front of block with no quilting

Back of block with no quilting

Overlap Quilting

Piece two or three strips of fabric onto the batting and quilt those pieces as a whole. In this block, the quilting overlapped two strips.

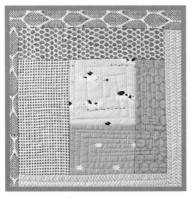

Front of block with overlap quilting

Back of block with overlap quilting

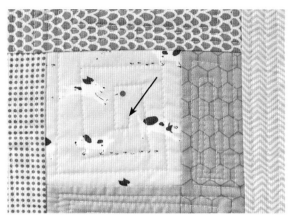

If you have quilting that ends in the center of a block or in a place where the last stitch cannot be hidden, tie off the top and bottom threads at the back of the block with a double knot. Or, backstitch a few stitches on the sewing machine.

TIP · · · · · · · · · · · · · ·

Quilting wavy lines is easy! Use a regular presser foot and set the machine on a straight stitch. As you start sewing, guide the block in a back-and-forth motion to make a wavy line. It helps to grip the left and right sides of the block, as if you were turning a steering wheel, as you guide the block back and forth.

In this example of overlap quilting on a large scale, the first 2 pieced strips were quilted with wavy lines running horizontally (across the seams) through both pieces. The last 2 strips were quilted with wavy lines running vertically.

Back of a block with wavy overlap quilting

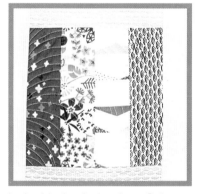

In this block, which is from *Salmon Run* (page 47), I pieced 4 center strips onto the batting first and used a straight machine stitch to quilt echoed arches over all 4 strips. I pieced and quilted the surrounding strips individually with straight lines.

Individual Quilting

Quilt each strip individually right after you sew it onto the block. In most cases, the quilting is simple straight lines parallel to the seam. See Making a Log Cabin–Style Block (page 18).

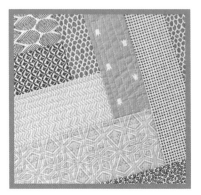

Front of block with individual quilting

Back of block with individual quilting

Combination Quilting

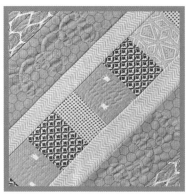

This block has a combination of straight-line quilting, no quilting (yellow strips), and free-motion quilting. I did all of the straight-line quilting first and skipped the pieces where I planned to do free-motion quilting. When I finished the straight-line quilting, I switched to a free-motion darning foot and quilted loops on the pieces that I had skipped.

In blocks like this, I quilted the loops after piecing and straight-line quilting all the blocks.

In this example, I started with a free-motion darning foot to quilt hearts onto the center of all the blocks. Then I switched to a regular presser foot, added the rest of the patchwork strips, and quilted each individually with straight lines.

In blocks like this, I quilted all the hearts first.

TIP • • • • • • • • • • • • • • • •

To avoid the hassle of changing from a regular presser foot to a free-motion darning foot multiple times, I suggest doing all of the straight-line quilting first, or free-motion quilting first, on *all* of the blocks. Then switch the presser foot and go back to quilt the rest.

• •

Free-Motion Quilting Tips

If you have been intimidated by free-motion quilting, now is the time to try it!

- Start by ironing the fabric onto the batting. Then pin the fabric to the batting before quilting. Remove the pins as you quilt.

- Use small-scale quilting designs that complement the size of the block. Larger movements are harder to make and can cause the block to bunch up in the sewing machine.

Stippling on a small scale

Stippling on a larger scale. It works, but it is harder to fill in all the spaces, and the large-scale movement can cause the block to bunch up.

- Have fun quilting your blocks. This is another truly creative part about this technique. You can follow my examples to get started, or go your own route to make something really unique.

ASSEMBLING QUILT AS-YOU-GO BLOCKS

After you have quilted and squared up the blocks, you are ready to assemble the quilt top. Quilt as-you-go blocks can be assembled either of two ways: the first is to sew them together and clip the corners; and the second is to use joining strips, which look like sashing strips in a traditionally pieced quilt. You can use either way or a combination to assemble the blocks. For both assembly methods, use a ¼″ seam allowance.

Block-to-Block Assembly

Using this method to assemble the quilt is similar to how you would assemble a traditional quilt, with the following two exceptions:

- **Use an even-feed walking foot and always backstitch.** The even-feed walking foot will prevent the layers of batting and fabric from shifting and puckering. The backstitching will keep the seams from coming open during assembly.

- **Press seams open and trim at the corners.** Use a steam setting to press the seams open. Press the seams on the front side of the quilt as well. To prevent bulky seams on the quilt top, clip all of the corners of the seams.

Trim the seam at a long angle to remove bulk at each corner.

1. Sew the blocks within each row together. Press seams open and trim corners.

2. Sew the rows together. Place pins at each intersection to keep the rows from shifting. Press the seams open.

3. Press the seams again, this time on the front of the quilt.

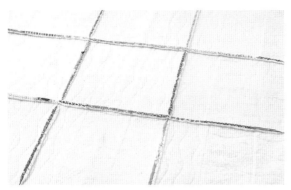

On the back, all seams are pressed open with all corners clipped.

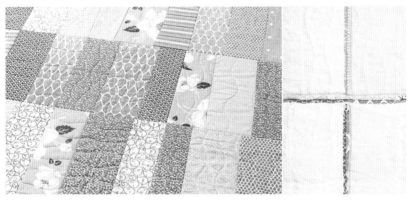

The front will look smooth, with all seams nice and flat.

The intersections at the back of the quilt will be flat with no bulk because the corner fabric was clipped and the seams were pressed open.

Block Assembly with Joining Strips

With this method, a ½″ strip connects the blocks. The look will be similar to a sashing strip. This method is a great way to subtly frame your blocks or break up a busy pattern.

Blocks sewn together with joining strips

Joining strips have no batting when they are sewn onto the quilt, so you do not have to press seams open or clip corners. After the strip is sewn to a block, press the seam allowance toward the joining strip, which will back it with batting.

1. Cut strips 1″ × the width of fabric. Trim a strip to the length of the block. Place a joining strip on top of the block, right sides together, and align the edge of the strip with the side of the block. Stitch together, starting and ending with a backstitch. Press the seam allowance toward the joining strip.

Press the seam allowance toward the joining strip.

2. Align another block along the opposite edge of the joining strip, right sides together, and stitch. Press the seam allowance toward the joining strip.

The joining strip should measure ½″ when finished.

After pressing, the joining strip will be backed with the batting from the 2 seam allowances.

3. Repeat Steps 1 and 2 to stitch each row.

4. Cut longer joining strips to match the length of a row of blocks. You may have to sew some strips together to make joining strips long enough. Repeat Steps 1 and 2 to stitch the rows together with a long joining strip between each row. You can place pins at the intersections to make sure the blocks line up.

Front of a quilt with joining strips

Back of a quilt with joining strips

BORDERS

1. Choose a border width. I often use 4″ finished borders (4½″ trim size) with 9″ blocks and 6″ borders (6½″ trim size) for 12″ blocks. Cut fabric strips the desired size × the width of fabric. Depending on the size of your quilt, you may need to sew some border strips together to make the border strips long enough.

2. Cut batting strips 1″ wider than the trim size of the fabric border.

3. Center and iron each fabric border strip directly onto the batting strips. Place just enough pins to keep the fabric from shifting.

4. Quilt the fabric directly onto the batting in any pattern you choose. Remove pins as you get to them.

TIP . . . .

Here's an idea. Keep the quilting minimal on the border pieces. You can add more quilting to the borders later when it is time to attach the backing fabric. See Finish It! (pages 102–109).

. . . .

I quilted simple wavy lines in this border strip.

5. Square up the quilted borders by straightening and cutting the borders to the trim size, which is ½″ wider and longer than the finished size. To trim, fold each border strip in half so that it fits on the cutting mat and align the fold with a grid line on the mat. Straighten the strip as much as possible. Trim from each side.

6. Add the border strips to the quilt top using the same technique as sewing the blocks together. See Block-to-Block Assembly (page 28).

Alternatively, you can use joining strips to attach borders. See Block Assembly with Joining Strips (page 29).

Attach borders to the top and bottom of the quilt first. Sew a quilted border strip to the top of the quilt and trim so that it is flush with the edge of the quilt body. Repeat for the bottom of the quilt, followed by the left and right sides.

MIXING TRADITIONAL BLOCK PATTERNS WITH QUILT AS-YOU-GO

Detail of *P-Patch* (page 100)

This quilt has a beautiful mix of abstract and traditional blocks, all achieved with quilt as-you-go techniques.

While many quiltmakers use the quilt as-you-go method to make improvisational quilts, you can make your blocks look as abstract or as structured as you want, or a little bit of both.

The traditional Ohio Star nine-patch quilt block is a good example since it is a structured block that typically requires premeasuring and perfect seam allowances to achieve perfect star points. In the following example, I pieced the same block four different ways, all using the quilt as-you-go technique.

Row-by-Row Method

1. Cut a batting square 1″ bigger than the trim size of the block.

2. Follow the pattern to piece 3 rows using traditional methods.

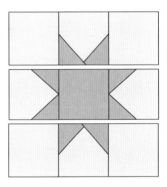

3. Quilt 1 row directly onto the batting. In this example, the middle row was quilted first.

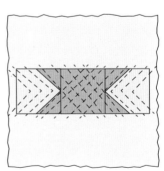

4. Sew the top and bottom rows to the middle row. Press them faceup and quilt each row. Square it up.

Block-at-a-Time Method

1. Cut a batting square 1″ bigger than the trim size of the block.

2. Piece together the entire block using traditional methods.

3. Place the block on the batting square and quilt it directly onto the batting.

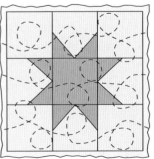

In this example, I quilted loops using free-motion quilting. (I recommend quilting at a smaller scale than I did here.) See Free-Motion Quilting Tips (page 27).

Patch-by-Patch Method

Quilt each of the 9 patches onto a batting square. Assemble the 9 quilted patches to make the block.

I used precut 5″ fabric squares, also known as Charm Squares. Cut 9 batting squares the same size as the fabric squares. You will not need 1″ extra batting to account for potential warping since the quilting is minimal on these small blocks.

1. Place print fabric squares on 4 batting squares. Place a solid-color square on 1 batting square for the star center.

2. Quilt the star center square and the 4 print squares directly onto the batting. Set aside.

3. To make a star point, place a print square on a batting square. Measure and mark the halfway points on 2 adjacent sides.

4. Cut a solid 5″ square in half to yield 2 rectangles 2½″ × 5″. Align the edge of a rectangle with the halfway points you marked in Step 3, with right sides together, and sew.

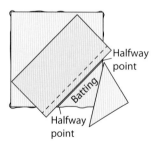

5. Press the rectangle open and trim the excess fabric. Quilt the corner onto the batting.

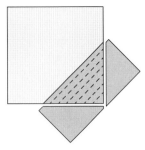

6. Repeat Steps 3–5 to add a star point to an adjacent side of the square. Quilt the new corner onto the batting.

7. Quilt the remainder of the block as desired.

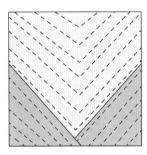

8. Repeat Steps 3–7 to make 3 more star-point units.

9. Assemble all 9 patches using block-to-block assembly (page 28).

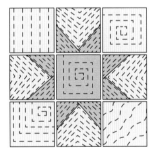

Improv Method

Improvise!

Follow the steps in the Patch-by-Patch Method (page 34), but do not measure the halfway points on the squares to create perfect star points. Instead, eyeball it and sew the rectangles on where you think the halfway points are. Or, you can purposely sew the rectangles at non-halfway points so that the star points end up being different sizes.

To see an example of this block and for more detailed instructions on how to assemble it, refer to *The Emerald City* (page 80).

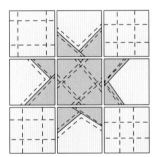

Imperfect star points make a one-of-a-kind star.

Projects

This isn't your typical quilting book with precise patterns and exact measurements. You can be as creative as you want while you quilt as-you-go. Because there are no precise patterns, no two quilts will look the same!

You are the artist, and the batting is your canvas. Embrace your inner creativity and make a quilt that's *all you*. Have fun!

Solstice Parade

These diagonally pieced blocks are easy to make, and the result is a colorful quilt that can combine all your favorite fabrics. I recommend using a bundle of precut 2½″ × 44″ strips. An advantage of using precut bundles is that every print is from the same collection, so your fabric colors and patterns will coordinate beautifully.

The Solstice Parade is a colorful and wild parade that celebrates artists but is mainly an excuse for Seattleites to welcome summer in their most natural state.

Quilt size: *45½″ × 54½″*
Block size: *9″ × 9″ finished, 9½″ × 9½″ trimmed*

*Fabric yardages are based on 40″ usable
width. Remove selvages before cutting.*

- **Fabric for blocks:** 2½″-wide
  strip bundle containing at least
  42 strips *plus* 4 coordinating
  ⅓ yard cuts or 5 fat quarters
  cut into strips 2½″ × the width
  of fabric. If you are not using
  precut strips, buy 5 yards
  coordinating fabrics in ¼ yard
  or ⅓ yard pieces, and cut it into
  strips 2½″ × the width of fabric.

- **Batting:** 1¼ yards of batting or a
  twin-size prepackaged batting

- **Backing:** 3 yards (or 1½ yards
  90″–108″ wide)

- **Binding:** ½ yard

Block Assembly

Solstice Parade block

Refer to Quilt As-You-Go Techniques (pages 16–35) for more
detailed sewing instructions.

1. Cut 30 squares of batting 10½″ × 10½″.

2. Using Cut As-You-Go Techniques (page 17), cut and place a
fabric strip exactly across the diagonal line that runs from corner to
corner on the batting square. To place the strip accurately, mark the
center at each end. Align the strip centers with opposite corners of
the batting square.

TIP ·

To quickly mark the center
at each end of the strip,
simply fold lengthwise,
and crease the fold with
your fingertips. Do this
for each end.

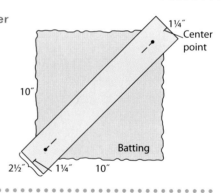

· ·

3. Quilt the strip directly onto the batting in any pattern you
choose. *Alternatively, you can piece all 7 of the strips onto the batting
first and save the quilting for last. I recommend doing it this way if you
plan to quilt a combination of free-motion and straight lines.*

4. Add a second strip. Press open and quilt.

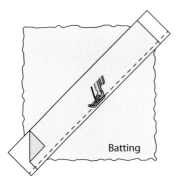

Batting

5. Keep adding and quilting strips until the batting is covered. Repeat Steps 2–5 to make 30 blocks.

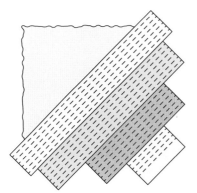

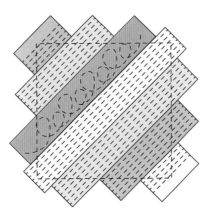

TIP . . . .

Remember that you can quilt in a combination of free-motion and straight lines. For tips on how to easily switch between free-motion and straight quilting, see Combination Quilting (page 26).

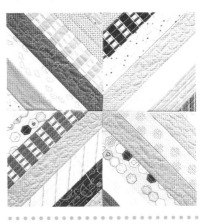

Square Up Your Blocks

Use the Precise Square-Up Technique (page 23) with a 9½″ square ruler or 9½″ square plastic template sheet.

If you use a plastic template, mark a 45° diagonal line going from corner to corner to help line up the block before trimming.

1. Place the block facedown and trim the excess fabric around the batting. Then, turn the trimmed block right side up.

2. Place a template or square ruler on top of the block so that the 45° diagonal marking is parallel to and as centered as possible with the initial center strip. Maneuver the 9½″ template or ruler around to ensure all sides are within the block while keeping the diagonal marking on the ruler centered within the diagonal strip on the block.

3. Trim all excess fabric outside the template or ruler.

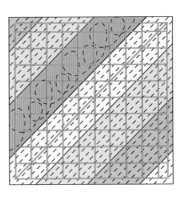

Quilt Construction

Refer to Block-to-Block Assembly (page 28) for more detailed sewing instructions.

1. Arrange the blocks in a 5-block × 6-row formation, turning the blocks so that the lines form diamonds. Sew together 5 blocks to form a row. Repeat to make 6 rows.

2. Sew the 6 rows together to form the quilt top.

Quilt assembly

Variations •

Use a solid fabric in *Solstice Parade's* center strip and watch the diamond pattern pop! Vary the strip widths to make it more interesting. See the photo of my son in the Introduction (page 5) for an example.

Break free from perfectly straight lines! Start with a wide center strip and piece additional overlapping strips at a slant. For more information on piecing slanted strips, see *Chief Sealth* (page 54).

Finish the Quilt

Cut the backing fabric in half across the width of fabric to yield 2 rectangles 54″ × width of fabric. Trim the selvages and then sew the rectangles together along a 54″ length. Press. Alternatively, cut a piece of wide backing fabric to measure 54″ × 63″.

For information about attaching the backing fabric and binding, see Finish It! (pages 102–109).

The fabrics in this quilt are from the Sew Stitchy collection by Aneela Hoey for Moda.

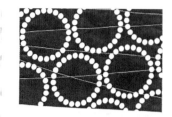

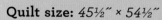
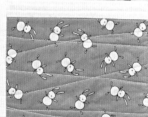

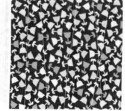

Rainy Days

Rainy days can be *very* good days.

Rainy days are a perfect excuse to stay inside all day—and quilt. Use that stack of fat quarters you've been hoarding, as this quilt design is perfect for showcasing your favorite prints. The block is simple and so is the quilting, straight lines only. Straight lines never looked so good!

Quilt size: *45½″ × 54½″*
Block size: *9″ × 9″ finished, 9½″ × 9½″ trimmed*

WHAT YOU NEED

Fabric yardages are based on 40" usable width. Remove selvages before cutting.

- **Fabric for blocks:** ¼ yard or fat quarter of 8 coordinating prints, *plus* 1 yard of solid-color fabric

- **Batting:** 1¼ yards of batting or twin-size prepackaged batting

- **Backing:** 3 yards (or 1½ yards 90"–108" wide)

- **Binding:** ½ yard

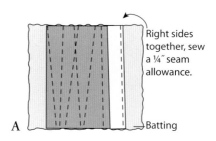

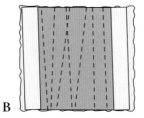

Right sides together, sew a ¼" seam allowance.

A

Batting

B

Block Assembly

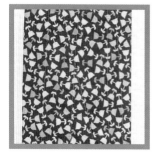

Rainy Days block. Make 30.

Refer to Quilt As-You-Go Techniques (pages 16–35) for more detailed sewing instructions.

1. From each print, cut 1 strip 7½" × width of fabric. Subcut into 4 rectangles 7½" × 10" to yield 32 rectangles. You will have 2 left over. (If you're using fat quarters, cut 2 strips 10" each and then subcut into 4 rectangles 7½" × 10".)

2. From the solid-color fabric, cut 15 strips 2" × the width of fabric. Subcut into 60 strips measuring 2" × 10".

3. Cut 30 batting squares 10" × 10".

4. Place a 7½" × 10" rectangle on the center of a batting square. Quilt it directly to the batting however you choose.

5. Sew a 2" × 10" solid strip to one side of the center rectangle. Press the new strip open and quilt. **Fig. A**

6. Repeat Step 5 to add a solid strip to the opposite side of the center rectangle. **Fig. B**

7. Repeat Steps 4–6 to make 30 blocks.

Square Up Your Blocks

Use the Improvisational Square-Up Technique (page 22) with a 9½" square ruler. To achieve the subtle "askew" look, simply position the ruler off center and tilt at a slight slant.

Quilt Construction

Refer to Block-to-Block Assembly (page 28) for more detailed sewing instructions.

1. Arrange the blocks in a 5-block × 6-row formation, alternating the direction of every other block. Sew 5 blocks together to form a row. Repeat to make 6 rows.

2. Sew the 6 rows together to form the quilt top.

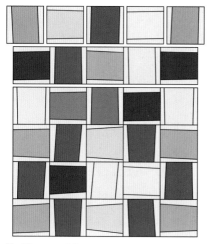

Quilt assembly

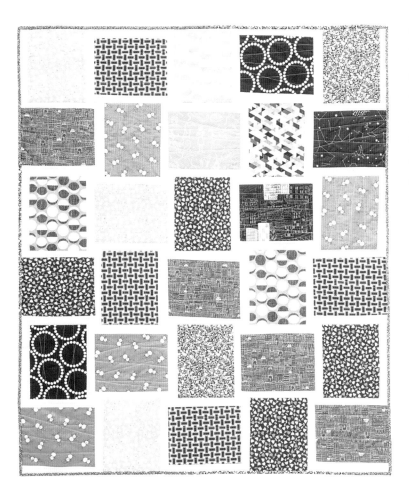

Finish the Quilt

Cut the backing fabric in half across the width of fabric to yield 2 rectangles 54″ × width of fabric. Trim the selvages and then sew the rectangles together along a 54″ length. Press. Alternatively, cut a piece of wide backing fabric to measure 54″ × 62″.

For information about attaching the backing fabric and binding, see Finish It! (pages 102–109).

Variations

In this version of *Rainy Days*, I replaced the solid rectangle in the center with patchwork. Piece the shorter vertical strips in the center first. Add the top and bottom strips, followed by the solid white strips on the sides.

Salmon Run, made by Jera Brandvig, 2013

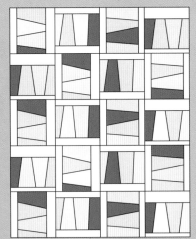

For another interesting effect, put slanted strips in the center of the block, similar to *Chief Sealth* (page 54). Alternate the block direction as you assemble the quilt.

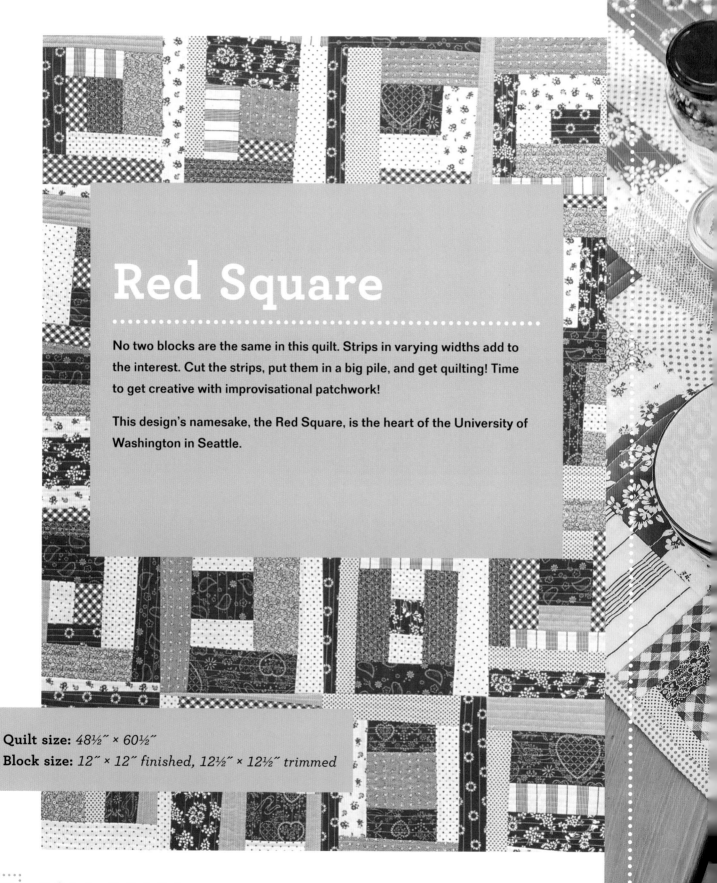

Red Square

No two blocks are the same in this quilt. Strips in varying widths add to the interest. Cut the strips, put them in a big pile, and get quilting! Time to get creative with improvisational patchwork!

This design's namesake, the Red Square, is the heart of the University of Washington in Seattle.

Quilt size: *48½″ × 60½″*
Block size: *12″ × 12″ finished, 12½″ × 12½″ trimmed*

WHAT YOU NEED

Fabric yardages are based on 40" usable width. Remove selvages before cutting.

- **Fabric for blocks:** 3½ yards assorted coordinating fabrics or 14 fat quarters

- **Batting:** 1½ yards of batting or twin-size prepackaged batting

- **Backing:** 3 yards (or 1½ yards 90"–108" wide)

- **Binding:** ½ yard

Block Assembly

Red Square block. Make 20.

Refer to Quilt As-You-Go Techniques (pages 16–35) for more detailed sewing instructions.

This block is similar to the one in Making a Log Cabin–Style Block (page 18), except you can add strips to any side of the patchwork and in no particular order.

1. Cut print fabric into strips 2"–5" × the width of fabric. Put all the strips in a big pile. For the most variety, choose strips at random.

2. Cut 20 batting squares 13½" × 13½".

3. Using Cut As-You-Go Techniques (page 17), from the first fabric strip, snip off a square or rectangle and quilt it directly onto a batting square. You can place the first piece wherever you want within the batting.

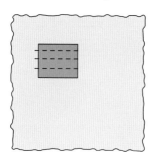

I chose individual quilting (page 26) using straight lines.

4. Sew the next strip to any side of the initial piece. Press open and quilt.

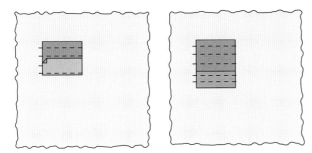

5. Sew a third strip to any side of the first 2 strips. Press open and quilt.

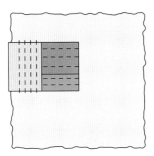

6. Continue to add and quilt strips until the entire batting square is covered.

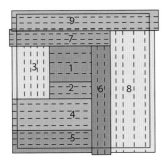

In this sample block, the first piece was placed off-center. All additional pieces were added in no particular order, which allows each block to be truly unique.

7. Repeat Steps 3–6 to make 20 blocks.

TIP ·

When piecing the fabric, alternate from light to dark prints, as well as small-scale to large-scale prints. The variation will allow your fabrics to complement one another.

· ·

Square Up Your Blocks

Use the Improvisational Square-Up Technique (page 22) with a 12½″ square ruler.

Quilt Construction

Refer to Block-to-Block Assembly (page 28) for more detailed sewing instructions.

1. Arrange the blocks in a 4-block × 5-row formation. Sew together 4 blocks to form a row. Repeat until you have 5 rows.

2. Sew together the 5 rows to form the quilt top.

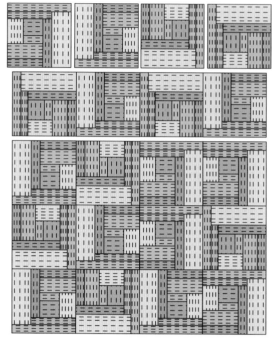

Quilt assembly

Variations ....

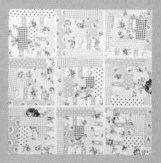

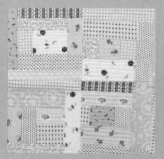

Try starting the first piece on the corner of the batting square and work your way outward, similar to a Half Log Cabin block or *Portage Bay* (page 92). Make the last 2 strips perpendicular to one another and the same solid color. Arrange the blocks so that the colored prints never touch.

Use joining strips (pages 29–31) to subtly divide the blocks. For this quilt I used a jelly roll to make Log Cabin blocks (page 18).

Here's another version of *Red Square* using fabrics that vary in color and intensity.

Finish the Quilt

Cut the backing fabric in half across the width of fabric to yield 2 rectangles 54″ × width of fabric. Trim the selvages and then sew together along a 54″ length. Press. Alternatively, cut a piece of wide backing fabric to measure 57″ × 69″.

For information about attaching the backing fabric and binding, see Finish It! (pages 102–109).

Chief Sealth

You can get really creative by piecing fabrics at slight angles to create blocks that look complicated but are actually quite simple. (It'll be our little secret!) The block in this quilt will show you the basics.

The fabrics in this quilt are from the Indian Summer collection by Sarah Watson for Art Gallery Fabrics. This collection combined with the block pattern (which reminds me of little tipis) inspired me to name this quilt after Chief Sealth, for whom Seattle is named.

Quilt size: *48½˝ × 60½˝*
Block size: *12˝ × 12˝ finished, 12½˝ × 12½˝ trimmed*

Fabric yardages are based on 40" usable width. Remove selvages before cutting.

- **Fabric for blocks:** 20 fat quarters or ½ yard each of 10 coordinating fabrics

- **Batting:** 1½ yards of batting or twin-size prepackaged batting

- **Backing:** 3 yards (or 1½ yards 90″–108″ wide)

- **Binding:** ½ yard

Block Assembly

Chief Sealth block. Make 20.

Refer to Quilt As-You-Go Techniques (pages 16–35) for more detailed sewing instructions.

1. From the coordinating fat quarters or ½-yard pieces, cut 80 strips 5″ × the 18″ length of fabric (parallel to the selvage).

TIP ....

Layer up to 5 fat quarters at a time to make quicker cuts. It helps to iron them first.

....

2. Cut 20 batting squares 13½″ × 13½″.

3. Place a strip on the left side of a batting block. Tilt it slightly to the right.

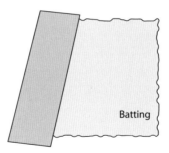

4. Add a second strip, but tilt it slightly to the left, leaving about 2″ of the initial strip exposed at the top. Stitch ¼″ from the edge of the second strip.

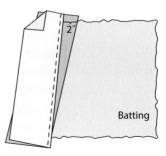

5. Trim the excess fabric from the initial strip and press it open.

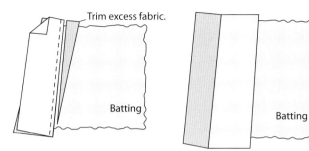

6. Add a third strip, tilting it slightly to the right and leaving about 2″ of the second strip exposed at the bottom. Trim the excess fabric from the seam allowance. Press open.

7. Add a fourth strip, tilted to the left and leaving about 2″ of the third strip exposed at the top. Trim the seam allowance. Press open to complete the block.

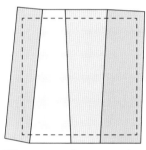

Tilt strips in alternating directions to make the block interesting.

8. Repeat Steps 3–7 to make 20 blocks. Quilt them *after* the blocks have been squared up. For this block I quilted simple straight lines to echo the shape of the strips. Leave at least ½″ unquilted around the block edges so that you don't cover up the quilting when you assemble the blocks.

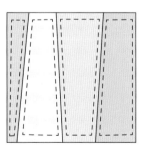

Outlining each strip highlights the block design.

Square Up Your Blocks

Use the Improvisational Square-Up Technique (page 22) with a 12½″ square ruler.

Quilt Construction

Refer to Block-to-Block Assembly (page 28) for more detailed sewing instructions.

1. Arrange the blocks in a 4-block × 5-row formation. Sew together 4 blocks to form a row. Repeat until you have 5 rows.

2. Sew together the 5 rows to form the quilt top.

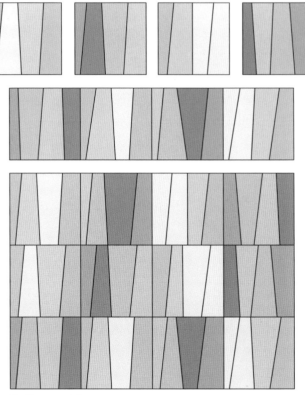

Quilt assembly

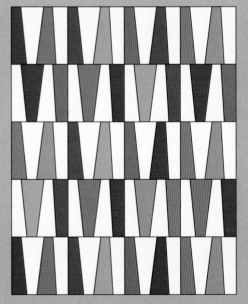

Try alternating every other strip with a solid color to make a lively *Chief Sealth* variation.

Make the strips narrower and tilted at random angles for a completely different look.

Finish the Quilt

Cut the backing fabric in half across the width of fabric to yield 2 rectangles 54″ × width of fabric. Trim the selvages and then sew together along a 54″ length. Press. Alternatively, cut a piece of wide backing fabric to measure 57″ × 69″.

For information about attaching the backing fabric and binding, see Finish It! (pages 102–109).

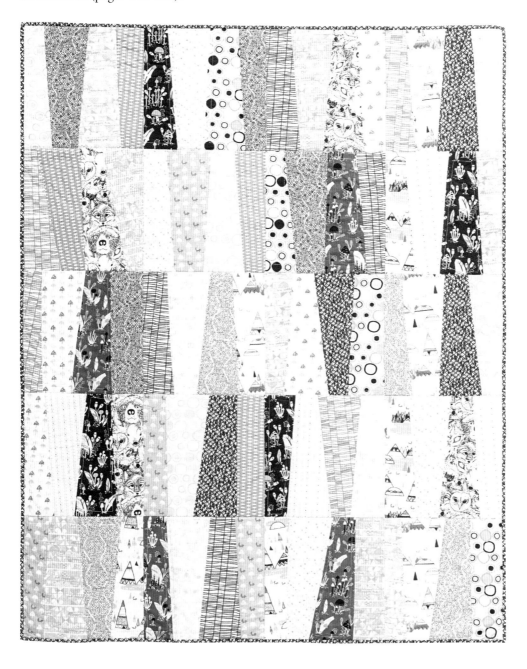

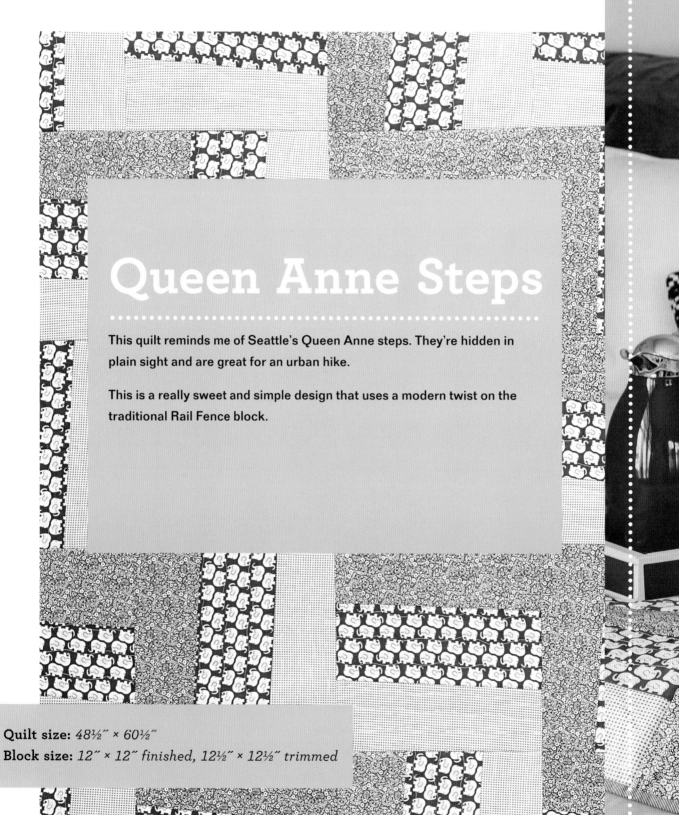

Queen Anne Steps

This quilt reminds me of Seattle's Queen Anne steps. They're hidden in plain sight and are great for an urban hike.

This is a really sweet and simple design that uses a modern twist on the traditional Rail Fence block.

Quilt size: *48½″ × 60½″*
Block size: *12″ × 12″ finished, 12½″ × 12½″ trimmed*

Fabric yardages are based on 40" usable width. Remove selvages before cutting.

- **Fabric for blocks:**
  1⅛ yard each of
  3 coordinating prints

- **Batting:** 1½ yards of
  batting or twin-size
  prepackaged batting

- **Backing:** 3 yards (or
  1½ yards 90″–108″ wide)

- **Binding:** ½ yard

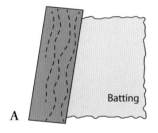

A

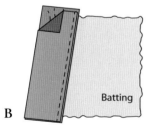

B

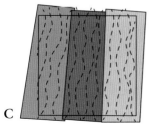

C

Block Assembly

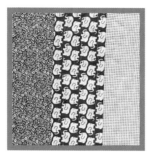

Queen Anne Steps block. Make 20.

Refer to Quilt As-You-Go Techniques (pages 16–35) for more detailed sewing instructions.

1. From each print, cut 7 strips 5″ × the width of fabric to yield 21 total strips. With scissors, subcut each strip into 3 strips approximately 5″ × 14″.

2. Cut 20 batting squares 13½″ × 13½″.

3. Place a strip, right side up, to cover the left edge of a batting block. Tilt it slightly to the right. Quilt the fabric strip directly onto the batting. I kept it simple and quilted wavy lines that run parallel to the slant of each strip. **Fig. A**

Quilt Construction

Refer to Block-to-Block Assembly (page 28) for more detailed sewing instructions.

1. Arrange the blocks in a 4-block × 5-row formation, rotating every other block so that the strips form zigzags. Sew together 4 blocks to form a row. Repeat until you have 5 rows.

2. Sew together the 5 rows to form the quilt top.

Start by choosing a print that you are in love with at first sight. This print will become the centerpiece of your quilt. Then, find 2 other prints to complement it.

4. Add a strip, matching the tilt of the first. Press open and quilt the new strip. **Fig. B**

5. Repeat Step 4 with a third strip, completely covering the batting. **Fig. C**

6. Repeat Steps 3–5 to make 20 blocks.

Square Up Your Blocks

Use the Improvisational Square-Up Technique (page 22) with a 12½″ square ruler.

Quilt assembly

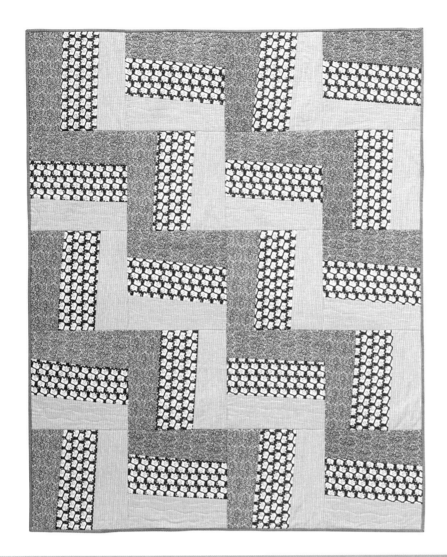

Finish the Quilt

Cut the backing fabric in half across the width of fabric to yield 2 rectangles 54″ × width of fabric. Trim the selvages and sew together along a 54″ length. Press. Alternatively, cut a piece of wide backing fabric to measure 57″ × 69″.

For information about attaching the backing fabric and binding, see Finish It! (pages 102–109).

Variations ....

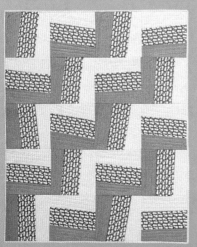

A different color combination and a change to how the blocks were positioned bring a new look to this pattern.

The Queen Anne Steps block arranged to form pinwheels.

Queen Anne Steps variation, 44½″ × 56½″, made by Jera Brandvig, 2013

Reversible Table Runner

This project is a great scrap buster and is really quick to put together. Choose a fun backing fabric to make your table runner reversible!

TIP

Customize the size of the table runner to fit your needs. Just remember to account for a ¼″ seam allowance and to cut the batting 1″ bigger than the trim size so it can be squared up after quilting.

Runner size: *13½″ × 34½″ finished, 14″ × 35″ trimmed*

WHAT YOU NEED

Fabric yardages are based on 40" usable width. Remove selvages before cutting.

- **Fabric for blocks:** ¾ yard of assorted scraps at least 16" long or 5 fat quarters or ¼-yard cuts (You will have extra fabric left over.)

- **Batting:** Craft-size batting cut 15" × 36"

- **Backing:** ½ yard cotton or home decorating–weight fabric

- **Interfacing:** Double-sided fusible interfacing, like fast2fuse Light. See Resources (page 111).

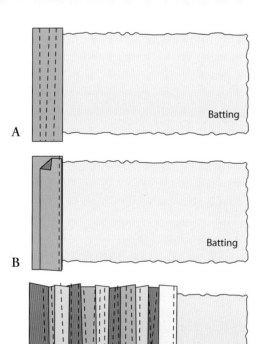

A

B

C

Table Runner Assembly

Refer to Quilt As-You-Go Techniques (pages 16–35) for more detailed sewing instructions.

1. From scraps, cut 16 or more strips 2"–3" wide that are at least 16" long. If you use ¼-yard cuts or fat quarters, cut 2 strips 3" × 16" and 1 strip 2" × 16" from each. From 1 fat quarter or ¼ yard, cut 1 extra strip 3" × 16". This will yield 16 strips total.

2. Align a fabric strip, right side up, on one edge of the batting. Quilt it directly to the batting. **Fig. A**

TIP •

Another option is to save the quilting for the very end. After the top is assembled, you can add individual quilting, overlap quilting, or allover quilting (pages 24–27).

• •

3. Add a second strip. Press open and quilt. **Fig. B**

4. Keep adding strips until the entire batting is covered. **Fig. C**

5. With the batting side up, trim off the excess fabric around the batting. At this point, you can add more quilting if you like. I did some additional overlap quilting.

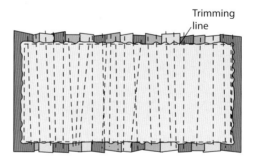

Trimming line

Square Up the Runner

Trim the runner so that it measures approximately 13½" × 34½".

1. Trim ½" from both short ends.

2. Fold the runner in half and align the fold with a grid line on the cutting mat. Straighten the runner as much as possible.

3. Trim about ½″ from both long sides of the runner to even it out. The runner should measure approximately 14″ × 35″ after trimming.

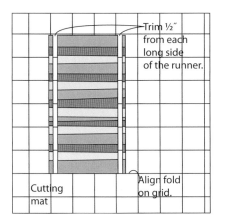

Trim ½″ from each long side of the runner.

Align fold on grid.

Cutting mat

Finish the Table Runner

1. Cut the backing fabric 14″ × 35″. Place the backing fabric on top of the table runner, right sides together, and pin.

2. Sew around the perimeter, using a ¼″ seam allowance and leaving at least a 5″ opening at the end. Start and end the stitching line with a backstitch.

3. Trim the bulky fabric in all 4 corners. Turn right side out through the opening. Use the edge of a ruler to help you pop the corners and the edges of the runner. Press flat on steam setting.

4. Iron the open seam allowance in ¼″ so it aligns with the rest of the seam. Use a strip of fusible interfacing to seal it closed.

5. Use a walking foot to sew a ¼″ topstitch around the perimeter of the table runner.

Variations

Use the table runner's assembly method to make matching coasters or place mats.

For a 4½″ square coaster, start with a 6″ batting square. Quilt as-you-go, using scrap fabrics. For block ideas, see *Triple Shot Sampler* (page 96). Square it up to 5″ × 5″. Finish it with a 5″ × 5″ backing.

For an 18″ × 14″ place mat, start with a 19½″ × 15½″ rectangle of batting. Quilt as-you-go using scrap fabrics. Square it up to measure 18½″ × 14½″. Finish it with an 18½″ × 14½″ backing.

Pillow Sham

The back of this pillow has an easy envelope closure. The design is made of strips pieced at an angle, similar to *Chief Sealth* (page 54). This block would make for a beautiful quilt as well!

The fabrics are from the Durham collection by Brenda Riddle for Lecien.

Pillow size: *16˝ × 16˝*
Block trim size: *16½˝ × 16½˝*

Fabric yardages are based on 40" usable width. Remove selvages before cutting.

- **Fabric for blocks:** ⅓ yard each of 6 coordinating fabrics for variety. You will have leftover fabric. Fat quarters will work unless you plan to make a pillow larger than 18".

- **Batting:** Craft-size prepackaged batting cut 17½" × 17½"

- **Backing:** ½ yard

- **Findings:** 16" × 16" pillow form

- **Lightweight fusible interfacing:** 2 rectangles 12" × 16½" (*optional*)

TIP • • • • • • • • • • • •

Customize the size of the pillow by cutting the batting to whatever size fits your needs. Just remember to account for a ¼" seam allowance and to cut the batting 1" bigger than the finished size so you have room to square it up later.

• •

Block Assembly

Refer to Quilt As-You-Go Techniques (pages 16–35) for more detailed sewing instructions. As you piece the block, scissor-cut strips in cut as-you-go fashion (page 17).

1. Using a ruler and pen, mark a diagonal line across the batting square as shown. This line will divide the block into an upper half and a lower half.

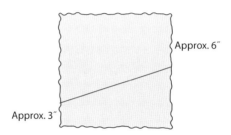

Approx. 6"

Approx. 3"

2. Cut a fabric square approximately 9" × 9". Align the square on the lower left end of the diagonal line, making sure it covers the lower left corner of the batting.

3. Cut a strip approximately 9" × 13". Position it wrong side up at a slight slant to the left so that it fans out. Before sewing it in place, preview its position to see that it will cover the lower right corner of the batting and overlap the diagonal line when attached. Sew. Trim excess fabric from the first strip. Press open and trim the excess fabric above the diagonal line.

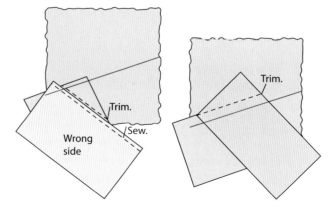

Trim.

Trim.

Sew.

Wrong side

4. Add a strip approximately 9″ × 11″ as you did in Step 3, making sure it covers the rest of the bottom section of batting. Press open and trim the excess fabric above the diagonal line. Also trim the excess fabric outside the perimeter of the batting square. Quilt the lower half as desired.

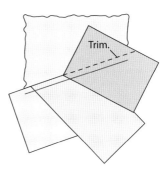

5. To fill the upper half of the batting, cut 3 rectangles approximately 5″ × 22″ each. Add a rectangle parallel with the diagonal line. Remember, the diagonal will be covered, so simply eyeball it. Sew and press open.

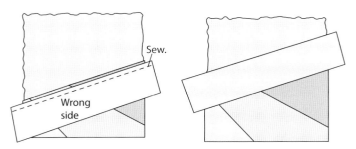

6. Add a second rectangle, previewing its position before sewing to be sure it fans outward and extends beyond the batting at both ends. Trim excess fabric from the first rectangle. Press open.

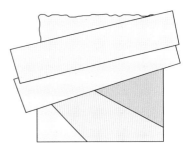

7. Add the last rectangle, positioning it to cover the rest of the batting.

8. With the batting side up, trim the excess fabric around the batting square. Quilt the top half as desired.

Square Up Your Block

Use the Improvisational Square-Up Technique (page 22) with a 16½" square plastic template and a ruler.

Alternatively, you can square it up using the grid on your cutting mat. Trim a little from 2 adjacent sides of your block to create a 90° angle in a corner of the block. Align the trimmed sides with lines on your cutting mat and trim the other 2 sides.

Finish the Pillow

1. From backing fabric, cut 2 rectangles 12" × 16½". If you're using cotton fabric and want it to be home decorating weight, iron lightweight interfacing onto both backing rectangles.

2. Turn under ¼" along a 16½" edge of both rectangles. Press. Turn under an additional 1". Press. Topstitch ¼" from each folded edge on both rectangles.

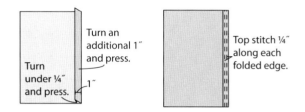

Turn an additional 1" and press.

Turn under ¼" and press.

1"

Top stitch ¼" along each folded edge.

Variation

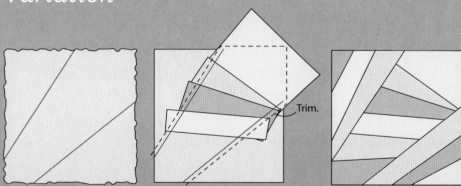

Trim.

Try dividing the batting block into 3 sections. Piece together the center section first, followed by the top and bottom.

3. With right sides together, place a backing rectangle on the right side of the pillow cover, with the top-stitched edge at the center of the pillow. Sew around the raw edges, starting and ending with a backstitch. Repeat with the other rectangle on the left side of the pillow.

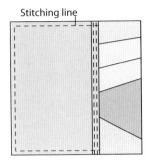

Stitching line

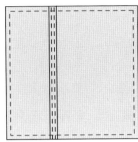

4. Trim the bulky fabric at the corners and turn right side out through the envelope opening. Press.

Ballard Blocks

This quilt comes together really quickly, and it is a great design for showing off some of your favorite fabrics! This quilt is layer cake and jelly roll friendly.

In Ballard, one of Seattle's interesting neighborhoods, you'll find a brewery and a hipster on every block!

The fabrics in this quilt are from the Nicey Jane collection by Heather Bailey for Free Spirit.

Quilt size: *60½″ × 72½″*
Block size: *12″ × 12″ finished, 12½″ × 12½″ trimmed*

Thursday
September
1 8

CITIES

REAL SIMPLE
THE BALANCED LIFE

Fabric yardages are based on 40" usable width. Remove selvages before cutting.

- **Fabric for blocks:** 10" × 10" precut pack containing at least 30 squares, or cut your own squares from 3 yards of coordinating fabrics, *plus* a 2½"-wide strip bundle or 2⅛ yards solid-color fabric cut into 28 strips 2½" × the width of fabric

- **Batting:** 2 yards of batting or twin-size prepackaged batting

- **Backing:** 3⅛ yards (or 1⅞ yards 90"–108" wide)

- **Binding:** ⅝ yard

TIP . . . .

Layer cakes and jelly rolls are yummy names for bundles of precut 10" squares and 2½" strips, respectively. The precut bundles contain fabric from an entire collection, so the prints always coordinate!

• • • • • • • • • • • • • • • • • • •

Block Assembly

Ballard Blocks block. Make 15 with the center tilted **right** and 15 with the center tilted **left**

Refer to Quilt As-You-Go Techniques (pages 16–35) for more detailed sewing instructions.

1. Cut 30 batting squares 13½" × 13½". If you plan on doing only minimal quilting, 13" × 13" will work.

2. Place a 10" fabric square, right side up, at a slight tilt on the center of the batting. Quilt as desired. I chose minimal quilting with straight lines.

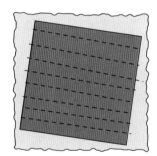

TIP . . . .

I suggest completing Step 2 for all 30 blocks (with 15 tilted to the left and the remainder tilted to the right) *before* moving to Step 3 to add borders. When you're ready to add borders you won't have to think twice about which way the center squares are tilted.

• •

3. Using Cut As-You-Go Techniques (page 17), add a solid strip to the top of the square. Press open and quilt 2 lines parallel to the seam. I quilted the first line ¼″ from the seam and the second ¼″ from the first.

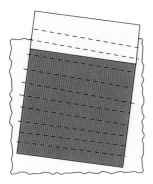

4. Repeat Step 3 to add a strip to an adjacent side of the first border.

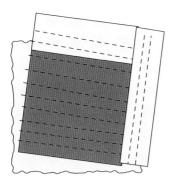

5. Add strips to the remaining sides of the block in the same manner, quilting 2 lines parallel to the seam for each.

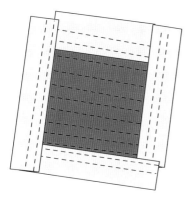

6. Repeat Steps 3–5 to finish the remaining blocks.

Square Up Your Blocks

Use the Improvisational Square-Up Technique (page 22) with a 12½″ square ruler.

Quilt Assembly

Refer to Block-to-Block Assembly (page 28) for more detailed sewing instructions.

1. Arrange the blocks in a 5-block × 6-row formation, alternating the tilt of the block center in every other block. Sew together 5 blocks to form a row. Repeat to make 6 rows.

2. Sew the 6 rows together to form the quilt top.

Quilt assembly

Variations ••

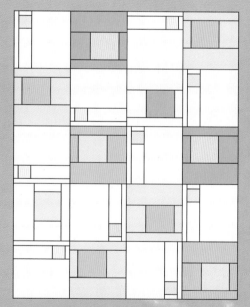

Try framing a *Ballard Blocks* square that is off center. To make it even more interesting, frame a big square and a small square. This simple block can take on a variety of looks!

In this version of *Ballard Blocks*, the squares are not tilted. Half of the blocks have solid white borders; the others are framed with prints.

Finish the Quilt

Cut the backing fabric in half across the width of fabric to yield 2 rectangles 69″ × width of fabric. Trim the selvages and then sew together along a 67½″ length. Press. Alternatively, cut a piece of wide backing fabric to measure 69″ × 81″.

For information about attaching the backing fabric and binding, see Finish It! (pages 102–109).

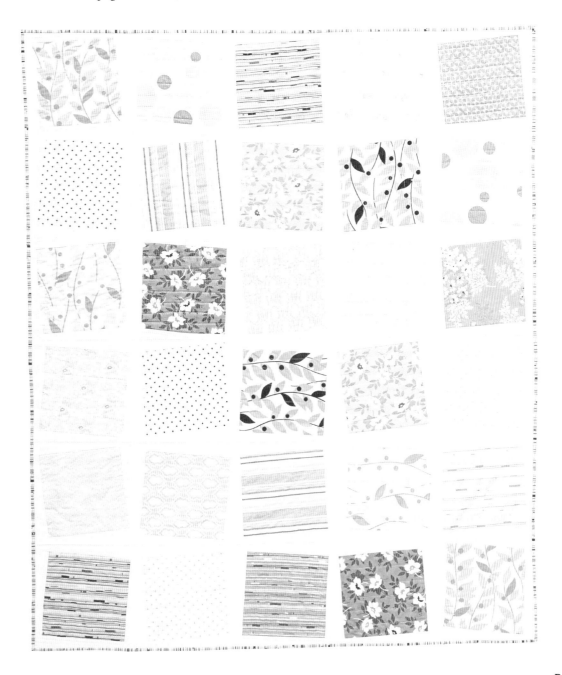

The Emerald City

Where land and sea meet is this city.

Ferries come and go. The Cascades misty glow.

The smell of the sea, and freshly brewing coffee.

Are all reflected on this city.

This is an improvisational take on the traditional Ohio Star quilt block. It is a simple quilt made of two blocks and is layer cake friendly.

The fabrics used in this quilt are from the Waterfront Park collection by Violet Craft for Michael Miller Fabrics.

Quilt size: *54½″ × 54½″*
Block size: *9″ × 9″ finished, 9½″ × 9½″ trimmed*

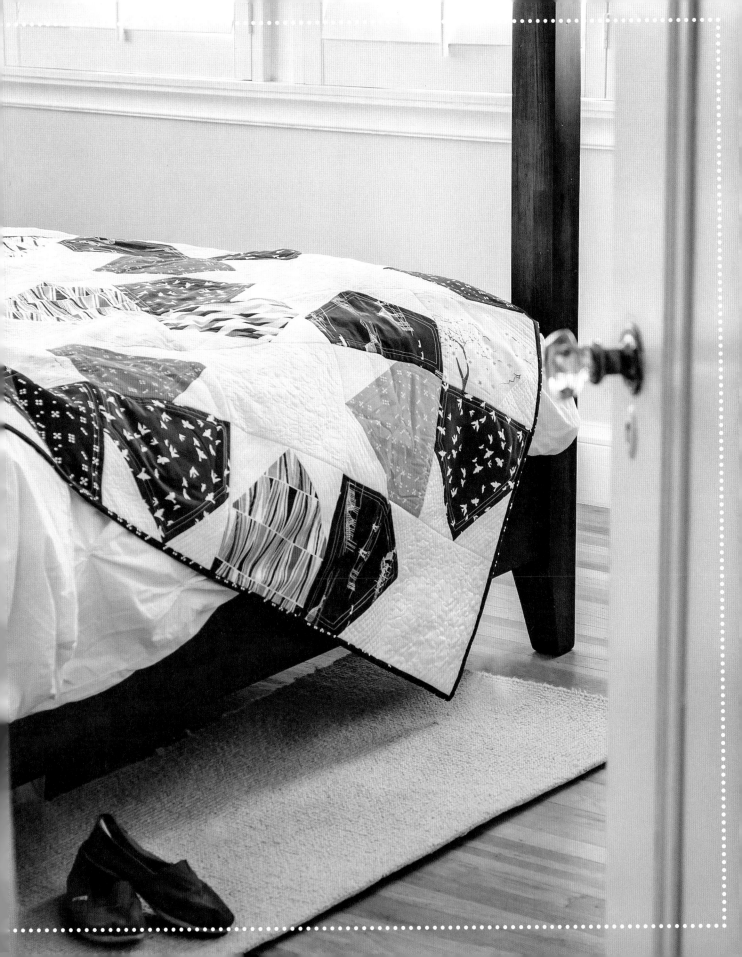

Fabric yardages are based on 40″ usable width. Remove selvages before cutting.

- **Fabric for blocks:** 10″ × 10″ precut pack containing at least 28 print squares, or cut your own squares from yardage, *plus* 3 yards solid-color fabric

- **Batting:** 1½ yards of batting or twin-size prepackaged batting

- **Backing:** 3½ yards (or 1¾ yards 90″–108″ wide)

- **Binding:** ½ yard

Block Assembly

Star Center block. Make 8.

Star Point block. Make 28.

Refer to Quilt As-You-Go Techniques (pages 16–35) for more detailed sewing instructions.

1. Cut 36 squares of solid-color fabric 10″ × 10″. Set aside 8 squares. Subcut 28 squares in half horizontally to yield 56 rectangles 5″ × 10″.

2. Cut 36 batting squares 10½″ × 10½″.

3. To make a Star Center block, place a solid-color 10″ × 10″ square onto the batting and quilt. I chose free-motion quilting.

Batting

For free-motion quilting, it helps to iron the fabric onto the batting. Place pins on all sides of the fabric and 1 in the center; remove them as you quilt. I recommend quilting small-scale designs. For more complete instructions, see Free-Motion Quilting (page 27).

4. Repeat Step 3 to make 8 star center blocks. Set aside.

5. To make a Star Point block, place a print square on the batting square. Sew a 5″ × 10″ rectangle at an angle over a corner of the square. Trim the excess print fabric under the corner and press the corner open. Trim the excess corner fabric so that it is flush with the batting square.

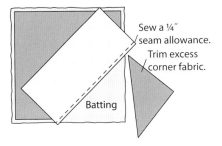

Sew a ¼″ seam allowance.
Trim excess corner fabric.
Batting

6. Quilt the corner directly onto the batting, using straight lines that are parallel to the seam.

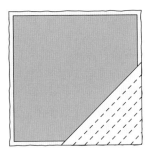

7. Repeat Steps 5 and 6 on an adjacent side. When you attach the second rectangle, be sure it overlaps the first rectangle at the V by *at least* ¼″. It is okay if it overlaps more than ¼″.

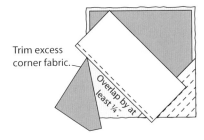

Trim excess corner fabric.
Overlap by at least ¼″.

8. Quilt the rest of the block. I chose to simply outline the remainder of the block.

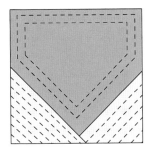

9. Repeat Steps 3–5 to make 28 Star Point blocks.

TIP ·

If you are using minimal quilting or want to outline the block as I have, it is easier to do this *after* the block has been squared up.

· ·

TIP ·

Purposely make the star points at different angles to make your stars more interesting.

· ·

Square Up Your Blocks

Use the Precise Square-Up Technique (page 23) with a 9½″ square ruler.

Quilt Construction

Refer to Block-to-Block Assembly (page 28) for more detailed sewing instructions.

1. Arrange the blocks in a 6-block × 6-row formation. Follow the quilt assembly diagram (at right) to place the blocks so they form stars. Sew 6 blocks together to form a row. Repeat to make 6 rows.

2. Sew the 6 rows together to form the quilt top.

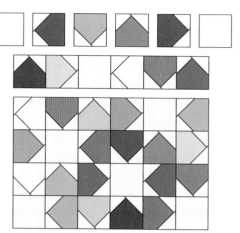

Quilt assembly

Refer to Block-to-Block Assembly (page 28)

Variations ••

Easily make pinwheels by adding only 1 solid corner piece instead of 2.

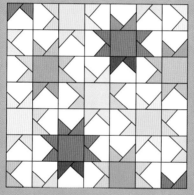

In this variation of *The Emerald City*, the colors are in reverse. The star points are printed fabric instead of a solid.

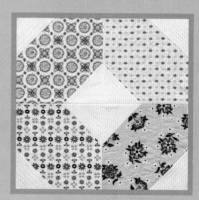

Try putting a solid corner triangle on opposite ends of a 10˝ square. To make the corner triangles, mark a diagonal line from corner to corner of a 5˝ square. Align it on the corner of the 10˝ square and sew along the diagonal line. Trim the excess fabric from the corner and press open.

I quilted the corners first with straight lines and used free-motion quilting for the remainder of the block. To square it up, I needed to trim only the excess batting surrounding the block. Due to minimal quilting, the 10˝ square kept its shape.

Sew along dotted line, and then trim excess corner fabric ¼˝ away from dotted line. Press down.

Finish the Quilt

Cut the backing fabric in half across the width of fabric to yield 2 rectangles 63″ × width of fabric. Trim the selvages and then sew along a 63″ length. Press. Alternatively, cut a piece of wide backing fabric to measure 63″ × 63″.

For information about attaching the backing fabric and binding, see Finish It! (pages 102–109).

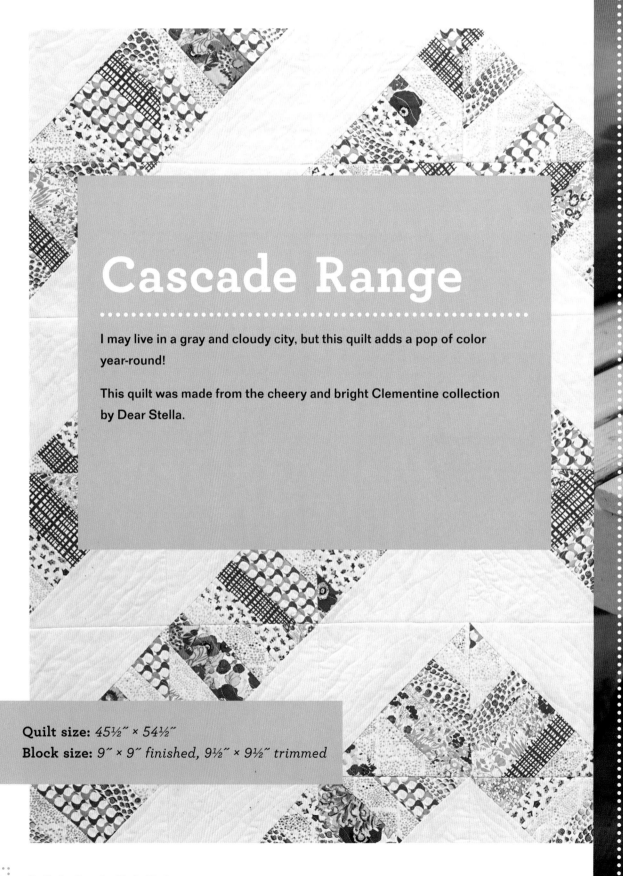

Cascade Range

I may live in a gray and cloudy city, but this quilt adds a pop of color year-round!

This quilt was made from the cheery and bright Clementine collection by Dear Stella.

Quilt size: *45½″ × 54½″*
Block size: *9″ × 9″ finished, 9½″ × 9½″ trimmed*

Fabric yardages are based on 40" usable width. Remove selvages before cutting.

- **Fabric for blocks:**
  ¼ yard or fat quarter of
  8 coordinating fabrics and
  1¾ yards solid-color fabric

- **Batting:** 1¼ yards of batting or
  twin-size prepackaged batting

- **Backing:** 3 yards (or 1½ yards
  90″–108″ wide)

- **Binding:** ½ yard

Block Assembly

Cascade Range block. Make 30.

Refer to Quilt As-You-Go Techniques (pages 16–35) for more detailed sewing instructions.

1. From each print fabric, cut strips 2″–4″ wide × the width of fabric.

2. From the solid-color fabric, cut 15 squares 11″ × 11″. Subcut each square in half diagonally to yield 30 half-square triangles.

3. Cut 30 batting squares 10½″ × 10½″. On each batting square, mark a diagonal line that runs ¼″ above the diagonal center line. This marking divides the batting in half diagonally, where one half is slightly bigger.

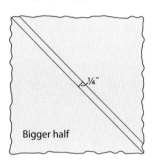

4. Use the techniques in Cut As-You-Go (page 17) to trim your strips. Align a strip right side up on the bigger half of the batting square, perpendicular to the diagonal line, with one edge of the strip touching the diagonal line on the batting.

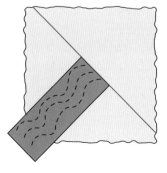

5. Add a second strip next to the first. Press open and quilt.

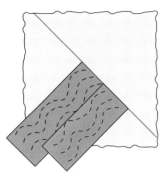

6. Keep adding until the entire half of the batting square is covered with quilted strips.

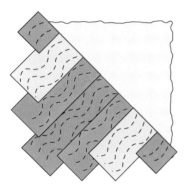

7. Position a half-square triangle to the diagonal line of the batting and stitch. Press open and quilt.

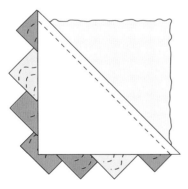

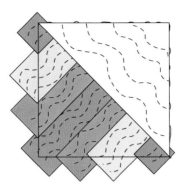

8. Repeat Steps 4–7 to make 30 blocks.

Square Up Your Blocks

Use the Precise Square-Up Technique (page 23) with a 9½″ square ruler.

After the extra fabric around the batting has been trimmed, align the 45° line on the ruler or template with the diagonal seam on the center of the block. Make sure all 4 sides of the ruler are within the block, and then trim.

Quilt Construction

Refer to Block-to-Block Assembly (page 28) for more detailed sewing instructions.

1. Arrange the blocks in a 5-block × 6-row formation. Refer to the quilt assembly diagram (at right) to arrange the blocks to form the design. Sew 5 blocks together to form a row. Repeat to make 6 rows.

2. Sew the 6 rows together to form the quilt top.

Quilt assembly

Variations ··

This simple Cascade Range block can be rotated in various ways to create completely different designs!

Finish the Quilt

Cut the backing fabric in half across the width of fabric to yield 2 rectangles 54″ × width of fabric. Trim the selvages and then sew together along a 54″ length. Press. Alternatively, cut a piece of wide backing fabric to measure 54″ × 63″.

For information about attaching the backing fabric and binding, see Finish It! (pages 102–109).

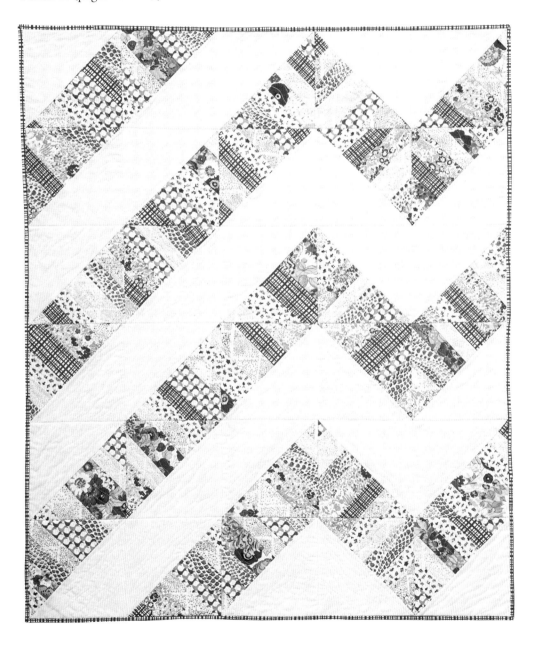

Portage Bay

This quilt is assembled directly onto one big piece of batting. In other words, it is not made up of blocks; but it is *one big* block! It makes a great baby quilt, wallhanging, or small throw to add a pop of color to your couch.

Quilt size: *30˝ × 40˝*

Fabric yardages are based on 40" usable width. Remove selvages before cutting.

- **Fabric for blocks:** ½ yard of 6 coordinating fabrics

- **Batting:** Craft-size prepackaged batting

- **Backing:** 1⅓ yards

- **Binding:** Use leftover block fabric or ⅓ yard

TIP • • • • • • • • • • • • • • • •

With the exception of the square or rectangle in Step 1, always cut strips along the width of fabric because you need to work with long pieces.

• • • • • • • • • • • • • • • • • • • •

This quilt was assembled on Warm & Natural's craft-size batting, which is a 34" × 45" sheet of needle-punched cotton batting. I do not recommend going bigger than this size. If the batting is too big, the quilt will warp from the quilting.

Quilt Assembly

Refer to Quilt As-You-Go Techniques (pages 16–35) for more detailed sewing instructions.

1. Start by cutting 2 strips 3"–5" × the width of fabric from each print. Also cut a square or rectangle at least 8" wide from one print. Eventually, you will need to cut more strips to finish the quilt, but I suggest waiting until you have completed part of the piecing. Refer to Step 5 for more details.

2. Align the 8" square or rectangle from the first fabric, right side up, with the edges of the upper left corner of the batting. Quilt it directly onto the batting.

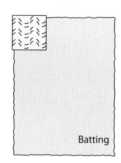

3. Add a second strip to the first, using Cut As-You-Go Techniques (page 17) and working along the short edge of the batting. Press open and quilt. I quilted wavy lines parallel to the seam.

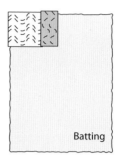

4. Repeat Step 2 with another strip, but add this strip along the length of the first 2 patches.

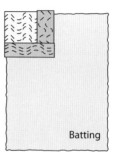

5. Continue adding strips in Quarter Log Cabin style, working your way out until the batting is covered. The quilt assembly diagram (below) is an example of how to add strips, but the number and width of strips is up to you. If you want to use fewer strips, cut the strips wider. If you want more, cut them narrower. Improvise as you go!

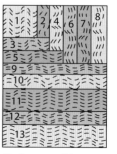

Quilt assembly

TIP

Remember that you can improvise the quilting as well. See Quilting Techniques (pages 24–27) for quilting ideas. If you combine free-motion and straight-line quilting, keep the scale consistent to avoid puckering.

Square Up the Quilt

The exact size of this quilt is not important.

1. With the batting side facing you, trim the excess fabric outside the batting.

2. Fold the quilt in half and align the fold with a line on the cutting mat grid. Straighten the quilt as much as possible. Trim enough to straighten each side.

Finish the Quilt

No sewing preparation is needed for the backing of this quilt. For information about attaching the backing fabric and binding, see Finish It! (pages 102–109).

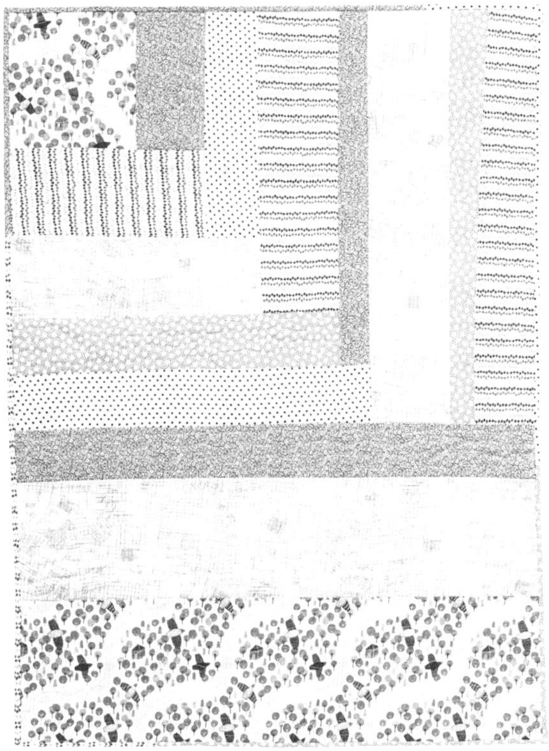

Variations

Portage Bay variations, 30″ × 40″, made by Jera Brandvig, 2013

You can make *Portage Bay* in colors to fit your decor or to match the occasion. Notice how the strips toward the outer right corner keep getting bigger. That is an advantage of improvisational piecing...if you want to just get it done, simply cut your fabric strips wider!

Triple Shot Sampler

Feeling too tired to quilt? A triple-shot espresso will do the trick!

This sampler quilt is made up of various improvisational blocks. Grab a precut strip bundle that you love and let your creativity take over!

I hope these improvisational-style blocks will get your creative juices flowing! I haven't gone into lengthy detail about how each block is pieced and quilted. Instead, I have provided the order in which the strips were assembled onto the batting.

Quilt size: *35½″ × 43½″*
Block size: *9″ × 9″ finished, 9½″ × 9½″ trimmed*

Fabric yardages are based on 40" usable width. Remove selvages before cutting.

- **Fabric for blocks and binding:** 2½"-wide strip bundle or ¼ yard of 9 coordinating fabrics cut into 27 strips 2½" × the width of fabric. Set aside 5 strips for the binding.

- **Border:** 1¼ yard contrasting fabric

- **Batting:** 1½ yards or twin-size prepackaged batting

- **Backing:** 1½ yards

TIP • • • • • • • • • • • • • • • • • • •

When choosing a jelly roll, think of the overall color scheme of your quilt. Softer colors blend really well right next to one another. With bolder colors, consider adding a border around each block or use joining strips when assembling the quilt to help break them up.

Depending on the design of your blocks, you can make 20 to 25 blocks 9½" × 9½" from a jelly roll that has 42 strips. Customize the size of your quilt by adding rows of blocks.

• •

Jelly roll friendly!

Block Assembly

Refer to Quilt As-You-Go Techniques (pages 16–35) for detailed sewing instructions.

Cut 9 batting squares 10½" × 10½".

The 9 blocks in this quilt were built by starting with an initial piece of fabric and then adding to it, so the patchwork builds upon itself around the initial piece. As I created these blocks, I didn't worry too much about the final design. The design of each block naturally took its own shape because of this approach.

I chose to quilt each piece individually (page 26) with simple straight lines.

TIP •

Don't spend too much time planning your fabric placement. Simply take a jelly roll, unravel the strips into a pile where you can grab strips randomly, and start quilting. Just go for it! You are not following a precise pattern, so the end result will be somewhat of a surprise. That is what makes this project so fun!

• •

Block 1

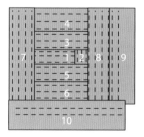

Block 2

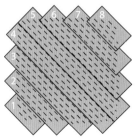

Try fussy cutting some of your fabric prints to frame an image.

Block 3

Block 4

Block 5

Block 6

Block 7

Block 8

Block 9

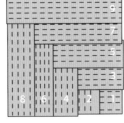

Square Up Your Blocks

Use the Improvisational Square-Up Technique (page 22) with a 9½″ square ruler.

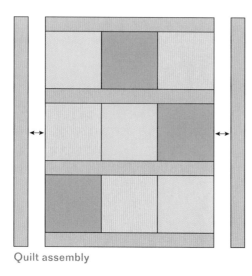

Quilt assembly

Quilt Construction

Refer to Block-to-Block Assembly (page 28) for more detailed sewing instructions. To learn more about how to prepare and attach borders, see Borders (page 31).

1. Arrange the blocks in a 3-block × 3-row formation. Sew 3 blocks together to form a row. Repeat to make 3 rows. Set aside.

2. Cut 7 strips of border fabric 5½″ × width of fabric. From one of the strips, cut 2 pieces 5½″ × 8″. Sew these to one end of 2 border strips to make extended-length borders. Cut 6 batting strips 5½″ × length of borders. Quilt the border fabric strips directly onto the batting strips. Trim each strip to 4½″ wide.

3. Trim the 4 regular-length quilted border strips to the length of a row. This should be 27½″, but if your row measurement is different, trim the border to match. Add a border between each row and at the top and bottom.

4. Trim the 2 extended-length border strips to fit the sides of the quilt. This should be 43½″, but if your quilt measurement is different, trim the borders to match. Sew the strips to the left and right sides of the quilt.

Variations ....

This sampler quilt, made by my friend and fellow fabri-holic, is the perfect example of how creative you can be with the quilt as-you-go technique. Notice the mix of abstract and traditional blocks. Tiffany didn't follow any precise patterns—this is pure creativity! Tiffany assembled the quilt using joining strips (pages 29–31), which really set off the blocks.

P-Patch, 53″ × 66½″, Made by Tiffany Behmer, Seattle, 2013

Finish the Quilt

No sewing preparation is needed for the backing of this quilt. For information about attaching the backing fabric and binding, see Finish It! (pages 102–109).

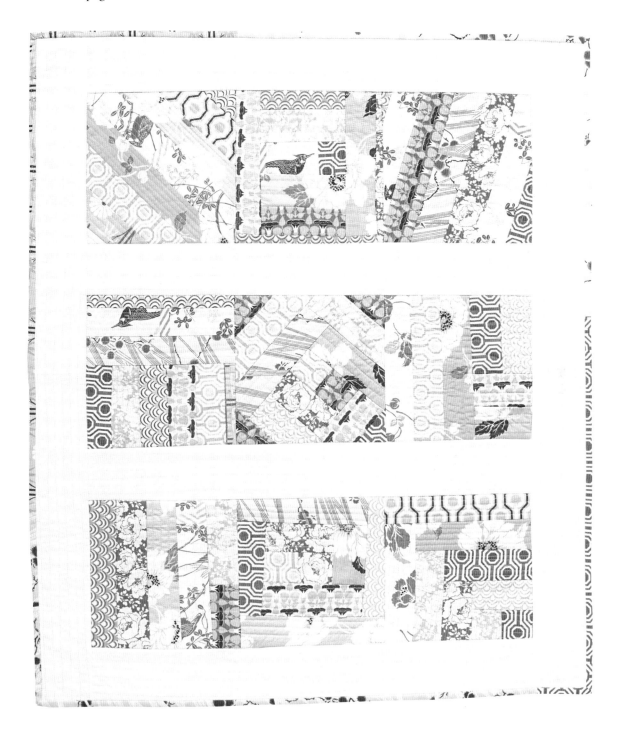

Finish It!

Your quilt top is done! Now you just have to add the backing fabric and bind it. This chapter will teach you how to add the backing fabric, as well as two ways to sew on the binding.

ATTACH THE BACKING FABRIC

The first step is to baste the backing fabric to your quilt top. With a traditional quilt, you would need to use hundreds of pins to keep the backing, batting, and quilt top from shifting while you quilt. Since your blocks are already quilted to the batting, you have to baste only two layers together, requiring far fewer pins. And, since all of the intricate quilting is complete, you will need to add only minimal quilting to attach the backing fabric.

TIP

Try using flannel for your backing fabric. It makes for a super cozy quilt, plus the flannel material naturally adheres to the batting, making it super easy to baste a quilt as-you-go quilt!

Baste

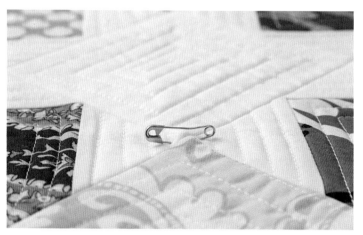

I recommend using curved safety pins when basting. The curve of the pin pops back up into the quilt for quicker pinning.

1. Start by placing the backing fabric, wrong side up, on a hard-surfaced floor or a large table. Smooth it out as much as possible and tape down all 4 corners. I like to use painter's tape. If your quilt is big, I recommend taping down the sides as well. The goal is to make sure the backing fabric does not shift around when you place the quilted top over it.

2. Center the assembled quilt on top of the backing fabric, right side up, leaving at least 2″–4″ of excess backing fabric on all sides. Smooth the top flat and pin it to the backing fabric. Place pins at each seam intersection and the ends of each seam.

In the following examples, X marks the places to use pins.

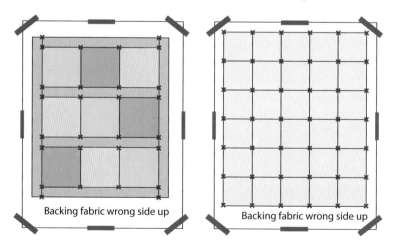

Backing fabric wrong side up

Backing fabric wrong side up

After you have completed the pin basting, you can remove the painter's tape and get ready to stitch the quilt together.

Attach the Backing Fabric with Minimal Quilting

Use an even-feed walking foot.

Since all of your intricate quilting is finished, you need to add only minimal and subtle quilting to attach the backing fabric. Choose a pattern and then either stitch in-the-ditch or quilt alongside the seams. Quilting lines parallel to the seam work well for quilts with joining strips between blocks.

You don't have to quilt every seam to form a grid. You can choose to quilt just the horizontal lines, vertical lines, or even zigzags. In the examples below, the red dashes show suggested quilting lines.

Stitching in-the-ditch is sewing directly into the seamline so that you can't see the stitches.

TIP

You can also try a simple tack stitch (X-shaped stitch) at the block intersections to quickly attach the backing fabric. This will give an effect that is similar to tying, but subtler.

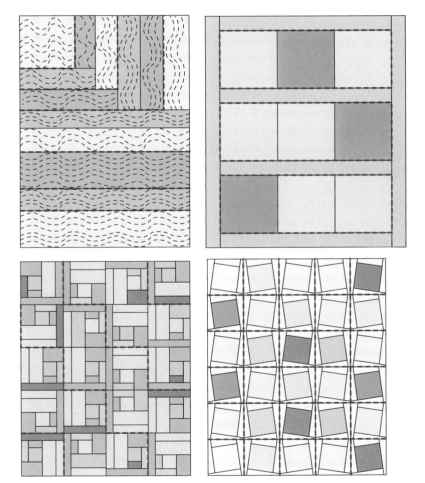

For quilting, use the seams as a guide to stitch in-the-ditch or quilt alongside the seams.

TIP

Sew slowly! If you have never
stitched in-the-ditch before,
start by sewing very slowly.
Once you get the hang of it,
you can speed it up as needed.

TIP

To calculate how many binding
strips you need to cut and
how much yardage you need,
add 10˝ to the total perimeter
of your quilt top. Divide that
number by 40˝ (the width of
fabric) to see how many strips
you will have to cut. Then add
2½˝ for each strip to allow for
the seam allowance when you
join strips diagonally. Check
to see if this changes the
number of strips you'll need to
cut. Multiply the total number
of strips by 2½˝ to calculate
the yardage.

Example: If the total
perimeter of the quilt top
is 210˝, you will need 220˝
divided by 40˝ = 5.5 binding
strips. Add (5 × 2½˝ =) 12½˝
for the diagonal seams to
make a total length of 232½˝.
Divide this by 40˝ and you're
at 5.8 strips. Round this up to
6 binding strips. Since each
binding strip is 2½˝ wide, you
will need 6 × 2½˝ = 15˝ of
fabric, which can be rounded
up to ½ yard.

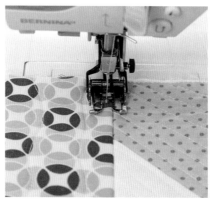

You can also quilt alongside the seam.
Simply guide the edge of the walking
foot alongside the seam.

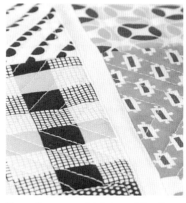

If you have used joining strips to
assemble your blocks, you can
quilt right alongside the strips.

Another option is to add additional
quilting to the entire quilt. For
example, if your quilt has borders,
you can wait to quilt them when
you attach the backing fabric.

After you have attached the
backing fabric, trim the excess
backing to be even with the quilt
top. Now you are ready to bind!

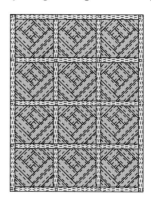

BIND YOUR QUILT

To bind your quilt, prepare the binding strips and sew them onto the
perimeter of your quilt. Finish the binding with a blind stitch by hand
or a machine stitch.

Prepare Binding Strips

1. Start by cutting 2½˝ strips from the width of fabric.

2. Sew the strips together with diagonal
seams to create 1 long binding strip. To sew
a diagonal seam, align 2 strips right sides
together so that they are perpendicular to one
another. Sew a diagonal line from the top left
corner to the bottom right corner. Trim the
seam allowance to ¼˝ and press the seams open.

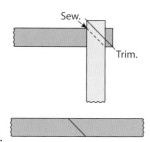

Sew.

Trim.

3. Press the binding in half lengthwise so that the width measures 1¼".

4. Unfold one end of the binding strip and fold one corner over as shown. Press. Refold the binding strip in half lengthwise.

ATTACH THE BINDING

Use a ¼" seam allowance to bind your quilt.

1. Starting with the diagonally folded end of the binding strip, pin the binding on a side of the quilt, away from all corners, aligning the raw edges of the binding with the quilt edge. **Fig. A**

Open the binding and sew 4" to 5".

2. Refold the binding. Start sewing the binding onto the quilt approximately 3" from the folded end, overlapping the previous stitching by at least 1". This will create a 3" open "pocket" at the beginning of the binding. **Fig. B**

3. Stop stitching ¼" away from each corner and backstitch 1". Lift the presser foot and needle. Turn the quilt so that the side you just stitched is now at the top. **Fig. C**

Fold the binding at a right angle so it extends straight above the quilt and the fold forms a 45° angle in the corner. **Fig. D**

Then bring the binding strip down even with the edge of the quilt. Begin sewing at the folded edge. **Fig. E**

Repeat for all 4 corners.

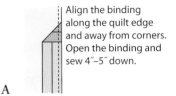

Align the binding along the quilt edge and away from corners. Open the binding and sew 4"–5" down.

A

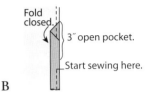

Fold closed.

3" open pocket.

Start sewing here.

B

End stitching ¼" from corner.

C

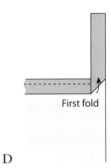

First fold

D

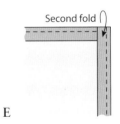

Second fold

E

If you plan to blindstitch
the binding to the back
of the quilt by hand, then
machine stitch the binding
to *the front* of the quilt. I
think blind stitching looks
the best, though it does
take some extra time.

If you plan to machine stitch
both sides of the binding,
start by attaching the binding
to the *back* of the quilt. With
this option, you will be able
to see a stitching line parallel
to the binding on the back of
your quilt, but the front will
be neater.

· ·

4. When you get to the end, you will come upon the pocket that you
created in Steps 1 and 2. Tuck the unfinished end into the pocket and
continue sewing until you cross over your beginning stitches.

Tuck the unfinished
end into the pocket.

¼″ seam allowance

Continue sewing closed.

FINISH THE BINDING

Fold the binding over the raw edges of the quilt back and pin. When you
get to the corners, fold the bottom edge of the binding straight up and then
pin the corners down to keep everything in place.

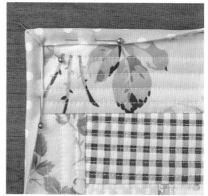

To finish the binding, you can either blindstitch it to the back of the quilt
or machine stitch it to the front.

Blind Stitch

This may seem like it will take forever. But once you get the hang of it,
it goes by more quickly than you would think.

1. Thread a needle with about 3 feet of thread. Don't go any longer,
or you'll get knots as you are blind-stitching. Start by hiding a knot
underneath the binding. Use the knot diagram (page 109) to create
a starting knot. You can repeat this a couple times to make sure it is
sturdy. **Fig. A–C**

2. To blindstitch, push the needle through just a few threads in the binding edge and then down into the quilt. Bring the needle up approximately ¼″ away from where you started. Repeat.

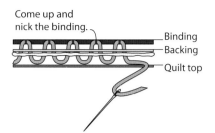

Come up and nick the binding.
Binding
Backing
Quilt top

3. When you get to a corner, stitch through the corner fold to fasten it. When you near the end of the thread, tie it off with another knot.

Machine Stitch

To finish the binding by machine, topstitch the binding in place from the front. Machine binding will create a top stitch on the front side of the binding and a line of stitches parallel to the binding on the back of the quilt.

1. Align the edge of the binding with the middle of your walking foot and adjust the *needle position* so that it is 1mm–2mm from the edge of the binding.

2. Stitch, guiding the edge of the binding strip along the center of the walking foot.

3. Slow down as you approach the corners. Remove the corner pin and replace it with the sewing machine needle. With the needle still down, lift the walking foot and pivot the quilt 90°. Put the walking foot down and continue sewing.

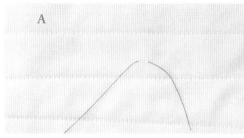

A

B

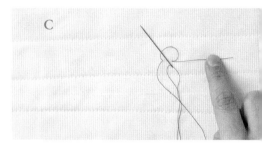

C

Knot diagram: (a and b) With your needle and thread, make a loop. Hold the tail of the thread so it does not slip out. Then (c) put the needle through the loop to create a knot. Repeat a couple of times.

Photo by Ben Brandvig

Jera Brandvig

About the Author

Jera approaches quilting as a creative art form and loves to bend the rules. She strives to bring out the inner artist in everyone and delights in the great sense of satisfaction that comes from creating something truly unique and beautiful. Jera lives in the rainy city of Seattle in a cozy home with her son, husband, and two furry "children." Her motto is, "Let your creativity *rain*!" Visit Jera at QuiltingInTheRain.com.

Resources

The first place to go for information and products is your local quilt shop. If that is not possible or they cannot help you, then try the Internet.

Supplies and Notions

Cutting mats, rotary cutters, and scissors
fiskars.com

100% cotton Essential Thread
connectingthreads.com > Thread

Pellon 100% cotton needle-punched batting and Legacy by Pellon 100% cotton needle-punched batting
pellonprojects.com/products-categories/batting

87.5% cotton / 12.5% poly Warm & White batting, needle-punched
warmcompany.com > Products > Warm & White

Walking foot for sewing machine
Your local sewing machine dealer

fast2fuse Light
ctpub.com > Tools, Notions & Interfacing > Timtex/fast2fuse

Fabrics

Art Gallery Fabrics
artgalleryfabrics.com

Dear Stella
dearstelladesign.com

Free Spirit Fabrics
freespiritfabric.com

Lecien
www.lecien.co.jp/en/hobby

Michael Miller Fabrics
michaelmillerfabrics.com

Moda Fabrics
unitednotions.com